Endorsements

A Time to Forgive is a critically important work, graciously shared out of deep, personal pain. Brutally honest, it is therefore authentic in its focus on the struggle to be Christlike while living through the massive trauma of life's darkest moments.

Is it possible to transcend human limitations and accept the gift of forgiveness, creating the same response that we hear so clearly from Calvary? Dr. Bigger eschews easy answers while providing profound biblical insights as to how that can be done. What a gift—all part of a moment of redemption that ends with forgiveness!

Robert A. Seiple, former president of World Vision

A Time to Forgive clearly and expertly explains forgiveness as an exercise of Christian faith. What makes this book special is the telling of the author's personal journey and the solid integration of that story with a research-based social science understanding of forgiveness into a coherent and compelling whole. I received important insights from this book. So will you.

Frederic Luskin, project director of the Stanford University Forgiveness Projects, senior fellow—Stanford Center on Conflict and Negotiation

This book is Darold Bigger's story of how God's miraculous gift of forgiveness penetrated his life. You won't find any step-by-step instructions for forgiveness here, but by walking this road with Darold, you will become more open to that divine gift.

David Neff, former editor-in-chief, *Christianity Today*

The reflections on forgiveness in Darold Bigger's rich and varied book show how important though difficult forgiveness is for us. And the book's frank and moving account of Darold and Barbara's response to the death of their daughter Shannon gives these reflections powerful validation. I know of no other book that draws from first-person suffering lessons of wide application more effectively than this one.

Richard Rice, professor of religion, Loma Linda University Author of *Suffering and the Search for Meaning*

In *A Time to Forgive,* Pastor/Professor/Chaplain/Navy Rear Admiral Darold Bigger shares in a most helpful way how he and his family dealt with, endured, and adjusted to a most horrific loss—the sadistic murder of their daughter Shannon. Through this heartrending narrative, the author tells how he and his family refused to allow that tragedy to control and thereby to destroy their lives. You'll find no trite clichés here—only raw feelings realistically communicated in a way that not only allows readers to identify with the Biggers' catastrophe but also to have a solid resource with which to manage their loss in a most helpful Christian way. Appropriately, Dr. Bigger's work allows God to use even this reprehensible evil for redemptive good.

Peter H. Beckwith, chaplain, Hillsdale College

This wonderfully inspiring book is a powerful and touching account of tragedy, of struggle, of humility, and of love and healing. It provides readers not only great insight but also hope that they too may have the life-changing experiences of forgiving and being forgiven.

VerNon Griffeth, chaplain, United States Navy Reserve (Ret.)

No matter what one's religion is, the most devastating loss is the loss of one's child. Each of us stands to be made more whole by taking in the intimate, honest revelations of one mom and dad's sacred journey through the seemingly unbearable challenges that struck the Biggers with the murder of their daughter Shannon. As you read this penetrating story, you will understand living, losing, forgiving, and loving more completely than ever before.

Bruce E. Kahn, rabbi emeritus, Washington, D.C.

This book helps me see that forgiveness is not reserved for occasions of great wrong but is a part of the Christian way of walking in the world. It makes the theology of forgiveness come alive in the daily reality of loving both our neighbor and our enemy. *A Time to Forgive* is for anyone who needs to forgive or needs to be forgiven—which is all of us.

Beverly Beem, professor of English, Walla Walla University

A person cannot read this new book by Darold Bigger without doing mental, emotional, and spiritual soul searching. First, the author tells a powerful and very personal story, and then he goes deeply and thoughtfully into what forgiveness is, what it isn't, and how knowing the difference enables one to survive a tragedy. A deeply moving challenge regarding love, evil, and forgiveness.

Fred Zobel, pastor, Little Stone Church, Mackinac Island, Michigan

A TIME TO FORGIVE

One Family's Journey After the Murder of Their Daughter

DAROLD BIGGER

Pacific Press®
Publishing Association

Nampa, Idaho | Oshawa, Ontario, Canada
www.pacificpress.com

Cover design by Gerald Lee Monks
Cover design resources from Dreamstime.com
Inside design by Aaron Troia

The author assumes full responsibility for the accuracy of all facts and quotations as cited in this book.

You can obtain additional copies of this book by calling toll-free 1-800-765-6955 or by visiting http://www.adventistbookcenter.com.

Library of Congress Cataloging-in-Publication Data:
Bigger, Darold, 1944-
  A time to forgive : one family's journey after the murder of their daughter / Darold Bigger.
    pages cm
  ISBN 13: 978-0-8163-5641-6 (pbk.)
  ISBN 10: 0-8163-5641-6 (pbk.)
1. Forgiveness—Religious aspects—Christianity. 2. Forgiveness of sin. 3. Love—Religious aspects—Christianity. 4. Murder—Religious aspects—Christianity. 5. Bigger, Shannon Marie, 1971-1996. I. Title.
  BV4647.F55B54 2015
  234'.5—dc23

                                                                                2014046432

February 2015

Dedicated

To all who need forgiveness and to all who seek to become forgiving persons.

Contents

Foreword

Admiral Darold Bigger and I were sitting in the chapel of the United States Naval Academy as a journalist interviewed us. While we were answering the journalist's questions, a crew of workers bustled around, seemingly unaware of what we were saying. Then, in response to one of the questions, Dr. Bigger began describing his journey to forgiveness after his daughter Shannon was murdered. As he did so, the bustling ceased, and everyone there eagerly absorbed his compelling words.

Forgiveness is something Admiral Bigger learned in the school of painful experience. His book is a must read for all who want to experience the benefits of learning how to pardon those who do us wrong. It is important because it will enable us to follow the example of Jesus, who forgave those who crucified Him (see Luke 23:34).

This book will prepare you to forgive those who have trespassed against you and to receive God's forgiveness, which is linked to our willingness to forgive (see Matthew 6:12; Colossians 3:13). Even more important: this book will help you cultivate such a spirit of forgiveness that reconciliation will become a habit. Eventually, you will be able to follow the advice Jesus gave in Matthew 18:21, 22; you'll be able to forgive people who wrong you "seventy times seven" (NLT)— the biblical way of telling us to keep forgiving until it becomes a habit. Finally, this book will guide you away from vengeance with the gentle reminder that payback belongs to God alone: "Vengeance is mine, I will repay, says the Lord" (Romans 12:19, NRSV).

In these turbulent times when violence and ill will seem so prevalent, we need Admiral Bigger's book to lead us to an ideal world where truth and reconciliation end the building of walls of rancor and retaliation. Read it and be transformed.

Barry C. Black
Chaplain, United States Senate

To the Glory of God . . .

This book is about forgiveness. It tells what my wife, Barbara, and I have learned about forgiveness through the murder of our daughter Shannon. Part 1 tells the story of her murder and the loss, grief, and comfort we experienced in the aftermath of that trauma. Part 2 sets out my understanding of what forgiveness is, what it isn't, and how it works. And part 3 presents an understanding of human life and relationships that I find particularly conducive to fostering a forgiving attitude and healthy relationships. Each part can be read independently and out of sequence.

In addition to the sixty relatives and friends I've mentioned by name in this book, many more relatives and friends have also been part of our journey since Shannon was killed. God places us in families and communities, and ours have been the source of immense comfort. Their conversations, notes, flowers, food, smiles, hugs, and friendship have sustained and stabilized us. They have listened, suggested, taught, shown, done, and prayed us back to stability. These people as well as several authors and editors have helped us journey toward experiencing and describing forgiveness. To them we are profoundly grateful.

Ever since Shannon was killed, Barbara and I have committed ourselves to sharing how good God has been to us. While this tragedy has brought us grief, relational tensions, and questions about the nature of God, our faith in Him stands firm. In fact, we have learned much in the aftermath of losing Shannon that has enhanced our confidence in God and our perceptions of human life. Our wish is that others might benefit from our journey, to the glory of God.

PART ONE

Our Struggle to Forgive Our Daughter's Murderer

CHAPTER ONE

Our Unthinkable Loss

Monday, June 17, 1996, dawned sunny and full of promise. The previous day—Father's Day—my wife, Barbara, and I had been in Portland, Oregon, where I had officiated at the wedding of Marta and John Stone—two of our daughter Shannon's friends. Unfortunately, Shannon hadn't been able to attend the ceremony. She was in Takoma Park, Maryland, finishing a one-year internship in the development department of Washington Adventist Hospital. Two weeks away from moving back west, she'd had to settle for our descriptions of the wedding and the reception. She had commissioned Barbara to take lots of notes so that she could remember every detail—every color and fabric, every movement and word and song, every smile and gesture.

On that fateful Monday I was in my office in the religion department on the campus of Walla Walla College,* the college in southeastern Washington where I taught. I was packing a summer term's worth of books, notes, calendars, and office supplies. The dean of the School of Theology was going to direct an archaeological dig in Jordan that summer, and I had agreed to fill in for him on campus until he returned.

In the midst of my packing, John Cress, chaplain of the college, phoned. He got right to the point. "Would you come to my office please?" he said. "I'd like to talk to you."

"I'm just moving my things to the theology department for the summer," I replied. "Could I come over this afternoon?"

---

* The school is now a university.

Shannon arranging flowers and feeding Hilary in Upland, California—1974

But John was insistent. "I have a personal matter of some urgency I really need to talk to you about right now," he said.

On my way to John's office I wondered what his "matter of some urgency" might be. When I got there, I found that Barbara, who managed the college store, had come too. She and John were waiting in silence when I walked in—John behind his desk and Barbara sitting in one of the chairs. When I had seated myself in another chair, John walked around his desk, looked at us, and said, "I have the worst possible news I could ever share with you . . . Shannon has been killed—murdered in her apartment."

That stunning announcement shattered our world. The look on John's face, the sag of his shoulders, the subdued tone of his voice all spoke to the seriousness of this message. It was no attempt at making a joke, no mistake.

All was quiet for an instant, and then everything burst into chaos. Barbara remembers feeling the blood drain from her head to her toes, as if her own life were ebbing away. I began to sob wrenching, gut-forced protests to this horrific announcement—as if my body were attempting to rid itself of those unwelcome words in the hope that, in doing so, it would also rid itself of the event they announced and all would be well again. But nothing changed.

I don't remember how long it was until the emotions that were so intense that they set us reeling subsided enough to allow us to talk. Then Barbara began asking questions and running through scenarios, trying to imagine how such a thing could have really happened.

John asked whether we would like to talk with the detectives in Maryland. Shannon had actually been killed in Maryland, literally across the street from the District of Columbia.

I said, "Yes," so John dialed a number, and a detective who had been at the scene answered. John handed the phone to me, and I spoke to the detective, who sensitively gave me the simple facts. That morning Shannon had been found on her bed in her apartment. She'd been assaulted and then tied up and slashed and stabbed to death.

How Barbara and I wished that something else had brought us to John's office—that something that had occurred on campus required our attention, that a student desperately needed our help, that Shannon was sick, or even that one of our daughters who were still at home was in trouble. But Shannon murdered? That was far beyond anything either of us could have imagined.

Shannon's last day

Shannon and her cousin Ava Steinert had spent the weekend together at Shannon's apartment. Having grown up on opposite ends of the country, Shannon and Ava hadn't known each other well. But during the ten months Shannon had been in Maryland, the Steinert family had been her lifeline and anchor. Shannon's internship had brought them close geographically, and they had become good friends as well as family.

The Sunday before we received the terrible news, all of them had gone to a United States Army Band program. That "Spirit of America" concert reminded Shannon of the time I had spent as a chaplain in the Navy Reserve—she enjoyed the rare occasions when she had opportunity to share those military ties.

As the end of Shannon's internship drew near, Ava was spending as much time with her as she could. She wanted to stay with Shannon again that Sunday night, but in only two weeks I was to load Shannon's things into a trailer and travel with her to her new job in Idaho, so she was using every spare minute preparing to move. She told Ava that she was tired and wanted to nap and then would spend the evening packing, so Ava went home.

Shannon with little sister Hilary posing for a Valentine picture for Daddy —1976

Later that evening, Ava punched in Shannon's phone number, but no one answered. That surprised Ava—she expected Shannon to answer because she knew Shannon intended to spend the evening packing. The answering machine didn't respond to her call either. Ava thought that strange too—Shannon always turned it on when she was going somewhere. So Ava decided to call again in the morning.

The next morning, Ava, her mother, Linda, and her brother, Owen, left for Providence Lab Associates as usual. Linda was a full-time employee of that company, and Owen and Ava had summer jobs there. Once at work, Ava tried again to phone Shannon, but the rings went unanswered. She told her mother that she still hadn't been able to reach Shannon, and her mother suggested that she try Shannon's work number.

This time someone answered her call, but it wasn't Shannon. The person who did said Shannon wasn't in yet and offered to take a message.

Ava asked when Shannon usually arrived at work, and she was told that Shannon usually arrived by eight-thirty.

When Ava told her mother about this call, Linda immediately phoned her husband, Don, and asked him to check on Shannon to see whether she was OK. Don took the spare key that Shannon had given them and drove to her apartment complex. *Perhaps she slept in this morning and got a late start,* he mused as he drove.

When he arrived at the apartment building, he saw that Shannon's car was in her parking place. Puzzled, he climbed the stairs and tried the door to her apartment. It was unlatched. Filled with foreboding now, Don wanted to leave. But he didn't. Instead, he pulled the door open and stepped inside.

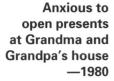

Anxious to open presents at Grandma and Grandpa's house —1980

The apartment was in disarray. But Shannon was packing for her move now, which could account for that. Don checked the living room and the kitchen and eating area, but he didn't see or hear anyone in those areas. Then Don went into the back bedroom. There he found the bedcovers neatly pulled over what appeared to be a person lying on the bed. One arm was hanging outside the covers.

It can't be Shannon, he told himself. Convinced in his mind and heart that someone else was in that bed, he pulled back the covers hoping to prove himself right. But the face he saw was Shannon's. Her throat had been slashed, and she'd been stabbed numerous times.

Fearful now that the killer might still be in the apartment, Don bolted out the door and ran to the apartment complex office. "Do you know Shannon?" he asked.

"Yes," the manager replied cheerily.

Then Don said, "She's been murdered!"

At those words, the manager grabbed her phone and called 9-1-1, and soon the place was filled with police.

The apartment complex had only one entrance, and a camera with the word *Surveillance* written in large letters on it kept watch of that entrance and the parking area. Fortunately, the camera was working that day. The camera's record of the day's comings and goings shows a white van—a vehicle that didn't belong to any of the residents—entering the complex. Neighbors said they'd seen the van parked behind Shannon's building and a young man loading some of her things into it. But they knew she was moving soon and thought perhaps the man had bought some of her furniture. They said they hadn't heard any suspicious noises.

Wittenberger and Turney, the Montgomery County detectives who were assigned to this case, were determined to find the perpetrator. The surveillance tape had captured the number of the van's license plate, but that license plate belonged on a different vehicle. The detectives drove all around the area looking for the white van, but they hadn't found the right van. And after more than eighteen continuous hours searching for the perpetrator, they were exhausted and ready to give up.

Then, as they sat at a stoplight on Georgia Avenue in the District of Columbia, a white van pulled up beside them. When the light turned green, they accelerated slowly so that the van would get far enough ahead of their car to enable them to read its license plate. The plate was the one they were looking for! But since these detectives were licensed in Maryland and they were now in Washington, D.C., they needed to have a police officer from the District stop the van. A radio call quickly accomplished that.

The driver of the van claimed he knew nothing about where it was on Sunday. He said his partner had taken it, saying he needed it to pull a caper. The man driving the van showed the detectives where this partner lived, and they obtained a search warrant.

Our family in Walla Walla—1981

When they entered the apartment, they found a young man named Anthony Robinson. He was watching Shannon's TV, and he had her flute, her camera, and her Walla Walla College video yearbook. They arrested Robinson immediately and took him to jail. There he told police and detectives numerous stories—at least eight, they told us. Robinson said, for instance, that he and Shannon "met at the mall." He also said she was giving him Bible studies and that was how he got into her apartment. And he said, "She disrespected me, so I had to kill her."

To evaluate these claims fairly, you need to know something about Shannon. She talked—a lot! She told her family and almost everyone else she knew all about the guys in her life, and there was *never* any mention of Anthony Robinson or anyone like him.

So how did Anthony get in? We've come up with several scenarios, but we'll never know for sure which is correct. However it happened, we know she would have been terrified when she realized that she was in trouble. The thought that during the last moments of her life she was so alone and so very afraid haunted us for months.

Notifying our family

The care with which our friends prepared to tell us that Shannon had been murdered amazes us. The Maryland police contacted our local police, who then contacted John Cress. He told the pastoral staff of the campus church, and after discussing the matter together, they decided that he should be the one to tell us about Shannon's death. John had grown up in the South and had joined the staff of our church while still in his twenties. He brought wisdom beyond his

Shannon—1983

High school senior picture—1990

youth and Southern grace and thoughtfulness for which we will always be grateful.

Henning Guldhammer, a pastor who had joined the staff of the college church while I served as senior pastor, offered to drive us wherever we needed to go. We decided that Barbara would go back to the college store to tell her employees, and then we would go to her parents' place. They'd moved to town just five days before—on Shannon's birthday—and still didn't have a telephone. Then we must tell Hilary and Rosemary, our other daughters.

However, the first person we saw as we walked out of John's office was Kirsi, a student who, three years before, had served with Shannon as a volunteer teacher on Yap, an island in the western Pacific. Barbara quickly asked me whether she should tell her, and we decided that she should.

When Barbara reached her office, she asked one of the employees to call the others together for a quick meeting downstairs. As the employees walked downstairs, one of them said, "I don't know what's so important that we have to have a meeting now."

"You'll soon know," Barbara assured her.

Of course, what we had just learned shocked Barbara's colleagues, employees, and friends. After an employee prayed for us, Barbara gathered her things and left.

Henning drove us to the home of Barbara's parents next. They had just moved to College Place—the small town where Walla Walla College is located—to be near us. Mom Messinger was surprised that we had dropped in at a time when we normally would have been working. But then she thought we had come just to see how the unpacking was going. She opened the door with her customary cheerful "Howdy do!" but when she saw our faces, she knew that something was terribly wrong. We told Mom and Dad briefly what little we knew at that point. They were dumbstruck. Their first grandchild was very special to them. Later, Mom would ask over and over, "How could this happen? We prayed for Shannon's safety every day."

Next, we headed home to tell Hilary. That morning Hilary had awakened ready to enjoy the first day of the very short vacation she was going to have between her junior and senior years of college. The doorbell rang just as she was getting out of the shower. She wrapped a bathrobe around herself and headed downstairs. The callers were John Brunt and Mel Lang, members of the college administration team. They told Hilary they wanted to speak with Barbara and me. But both of us had gone to work some time before, and we weren't expected home for several hours. Hilary thought their request odd.

College senior portrait—1995

The two men wouldn't explain further; they would only say that it was likely that we would be home soon. Hilary invited the two men in to wait for us there, but they declined her offer and waited in their car instead—which Hilary thought was also odd. A few minutes later Barbara and I arrived at the house and told Hilary that her older sister had been murdered.

Within hours Hilary's dearest friends were arriving, one having driven back from her honeymoon to be with Hilary. She doesn't remember crying much. Mostly, she just felt numb.

Hilary resembles me in some ways, but she is introverted and I'm more of an extrovert. She cherishes her private times and rejuvenates herself by spending time alone or with a very small group of select friends. She handles stress and tension by withdrawing.

When we told Hilary that Shannon had been murdered, she held her emotions in rather than unleashing them immediately as I had done. And when the house became a whirlwind of people, phone calls, messages, and visitors, instead of joining the hubbub, she called a couple of very close friends and then left to be with them.

My parents, Mom and Dad Bigger, who lived in southern Oregon, called us before we had an opportunity to tell them about Shannon's death. "Is it true?" they asked.

Dear friends of theirs had called, asking that question. A young staff member who was on campus had phoned her grandparents to tell them that they should arrange to have someone with Mom and Dad Bigger at all times during the next several days. She had heard about Shannon's death before we did. Of course, we were disappointed that we weren't the ones to break the news to my parents, but we knew that people were only trying to help. Later, we found out that many people had heard about the tragedy before we did.

As the news spread, the university administrators, who were also personal friends, came to our house wanting to be of help to us. Fortunately, they didn't ask what we needed; we couldn't begin to think about that. But they knew.

Some of them said they wanted to clean our house. Barbara has never wanted a housekeeper. She always answered my occasional suggestion that we hire someone with the words "I'd rather do it myself." But now, when our friends said that was what they wanted to do, she realized that she needed their help. So she showed the volunteers where she kept her cleaning supplies. I still remember vividly the sight of one of our vice presidents standing on our front porch and shaking our bathroom rugs. That was a gift of love!

Walla Walla College graduation —June 11, 1995

Within three or four hours of the time we heard the news, a bouquet of flowers arrived. We didn't recognize the name on the card and had no idea who had been so thoughtful and generous. Then it dawned on us: the sender was a neighbor we hardly knew—a clerk at a local store with whom Barbara chatted a bit when she went through her checkout line. What a gesture of caring!

Later that day, colleague and friend Bev Beem brought over a big pot of homemade soup, adding it to the many fruit baskets and vegetable trays that had arrived. I couldn't imagine eating anything, but when I looked at the clock and realized we hadn't eaten all day, I knew the soup was just the thing we needed.

Mel and Joyce Lang, friends who had lost a young son to a brain tumor years before, also came over. Joyce had taught Shannon in grade school, and they'd had a special bond. Like the others who had come to help, Joyce didn't ask what she could do. She said, "I want to take your laundry home and do it up for you."

Again, this was difficult for Barbara. She didn't want anyone other than herself to wash our dirty laundry! But she was practical enough to know that it needed doing and that she wasn't going to have time. So Barbara gave Joyce the laundry basket, and the next day she returned all the clothes clean and neatly folded. What a blessing!

Rosemary, our foster daughter, was in a driver's education class when we were told the terrible news, so several hours passed before she heard about Shannon's death. When she was told about it, she absorbed the news stoically, but I have no doubt that it devastated her.

Rosemary is from Yap, a ten-mile-long, four-mile-wide atoll in the Pacific Ocean 530 miles southwest of Guam. Three years before Shannon was murdered, she spent most of a year on Yap, serving as a volunteer first-grade teacher in the Adventist school there. Near the end of her stint, Barbara and I flew to Yap to spend a week with her. We met Rosemary during that week.

This young girl was already too well acquainted with trauma and its effects: when she was about six years old, she had seen her drunken father kill her mother, and while he served his sentence, Rosemary and her siblings were left to find a way to survive on their own.

Shannon was Rosemary's link to her home on Yap. No one else in Walla Walla knew the people and the foods, the villages, the customs

Shannon at her favorite place on earth—1995

Shannon's body being removed from her Maryland apartment—June 17, 1996

and the plants, the fish, and the birds that she knew. Being shy and self-conscious and worried about the adequacy of her English and wanting desperately to please us, yet being so far from all that was familiar and comforting to her was difficult enough. The loss of Shannon was a heavy additional blow.

After we had talked in person with all those we could reach, we called other family members from home. The next hours and days were a blur. This tragedy had a heavy impact on our extended family, but their response was equally profound: they rushed to Walla Walla to surround us. By car and plane they came, some from across the country, so we could all be together. They were and continue to be a strong, crucial part of our support network.

They, too, needed support. This trauma happened to them as well as to us. They also were victims, plunged into grief, mourning the loss of a family member and friend. They, too, experienced the increased anxiety imposed on us by this reminder that we live in an unsafe world. It hasn't been an easy journey for them either.

CHAPTER TWO

The Funeral

As parents, our first thought was that we should fly to Maryland to be with our daughter. The feeling that we were abandoning her by staying home in Washington State was nearly overwhelming. But we realized that our going to Maryland didn't make any sense. Shannon wouldn't know that we had come, and we couldn't do anything to help her anyway. What we really needed to do now was to determine the who, when, and where of her funeral. So we stayed at home and began the planning.

Since Walla Walla was home to Shannon, Barbara, and me, we decided to have her body brought here for burial. However, Shannon had established her own church home in Maryland as well, and the friends she had made there also wanted and deserved a service in which they could honor her. So we decided to have two services for her: a funeral in the college church in Washington and a memorial service in Maryland.

On Wednesday evening of that traumatic week, John Brunt took us to the airport in Pasco, Washington, where we would welcome our daughter home. When we arrived, we sat in the car by a fence and watched people leave the plane that we thought was probably the one on which Shannon had come. No doubt many of the passengers who had arrived on it were joyfully anticipating the pleasure of being welcomed by their loved ones. But our daughter lay cold and silent in a casket. The contrast was almost more than we could endure.

When the ground crew had removed all the luggage from the plane, they lowered a rather small white cardboard box, which was shaped like the stereotypical coffins seen in horror movies, onto the back of a golf cart. Then, instead of going to the passenger terminal, they headed toward the cargo building. We couldn't help but notice the implication. (When the police were collecting everything that might be used as evidence in the trial that would eventually be held, they put it all in what looked like large plastic trash bags. And when they took Shannon to the morgue, they put her in a plastic body bag. Barbara says that even now, when she catches a glimpse of those bags in a photo or a video, she's bothered by the thought that *our daughter* was relegated to one of those bags.)

The cart that carried Shannon to the cargo building did bring a bit of humor into what otherwise was terribly sad. As it bounced along the tarmac, we chuckled at the thought that Shannon would have loved that ride. It was almost like something you'd experience in an amusement park!

The hearse was waiting for us near the cargo building. When Shannon's casket had been loaded into it, Barbara and I chose to ride with her one more time, so we sat in the front seat of the hearse with the funeral director.

As we headed toward College Place, I put my arm around Barbara. Then every once in a while I would reach back and touch the box that Shannon was in. When I did, the thought came to mind that I was touching two women whom I loved deeply—but one was warm and alive, and the other was cold and still in a cardboard box. Tears streamed down Barbara's face and mine as we wished we really could touch Shannon—could touch a living Shannon. We wished that what we knew to be true wasn't. Our Shannon was so close, yet so far away. I felt inconsolable, as though grief had opened all the pores of my body, and everything inside was draining out, leaving me an empty shell. By the time we got home, I was exhausted.

The funeral home personnel told us that they could hide the wounds Shannon had suffered, so we chose to have an open-casket service. That posed a problem. We had no access to Shannon's clothes because all of them were in her apartment, which now was a crime scene that no one other than the local authorities could enter. Consequently, Barbara and Hilary had to buy something for Shannon to wear at the funeral. So, Hilary and Barbara went shopping. They found the perfect little navy-blue suit with white trim and a scarf that would cover what little could still be seen of the wounds on her neck, and they delivered the outfit to the funeral home. What a surreal experience!

Planning

We spent Tuesday and Wednesday planning Shannon's funeral, deciding whom we wanted to speak at the service, whom we'd ask to provide the music, and so forth. Some choices were easy, and others more difficult.

John Cress and Henning Guldhammer were helping us plan the service; but as we worked on it, my caretaker and pastor self kicked in and I started laying out all the details of the service: where we would meet before the service began, where each participant would sit, how long this song should be, when that person would step up to the microphone, and on and on. For many years, I had conducted funerals and taken care of families during their times of loss, and now I was finding it extremely difficult to let other people care for my family and me.

Eventually, Henning and John asked Barbara to encourage me to let them handle the details. She raised the issue as we were preparing to go to bed. She reminded me that I had mentored these pastors for several years and they knew how to plan a funeral service, so I needed to let them be the caregivers now. I knew that, but right then I desperately wanted to have control over every part of my life.

The viewing was held at the funeral chapel on Thursday evening. As I remember it, Shannon's viewing began at seven o'clock. We arrived early so we could see Shannon before anyone other than family was allowed in the room.

When Barbara and I walked in with our parents, with Hilary and Rosemary and aunts, uncles, and cousins, I went to the casket, fell to my knees, and wailed. Barbara says she had never before heard such a sound—she thought I had collapsed from grief. I *was* overcome at the sight of our firstborn—she looked so still and white. Seeing her for the first time since her death was unspeakably difficult. I didn't know people could cry so much. We cried until we literally ran out of tears—something we had never done before.

Eventually, the doors were opened to people who wanted to greet us and share our tears. Usually, no more than a handful of people come to a viewing, but that night young and old streamed into the main funeral parlor chapel. (Usually, a side room is adequate.) For more than two hours, they passed by Shannon's casket in a continuous line. Many were Shannon's classmates. Some were people whom we hadn't seen in years. All of them were very broken up.

The funeral was held on the next day, Friday. Barbara wore a dress that

Shannon and Hilary had given her several years before as a Mother's Day gift.

Riding to the church in the funeral home's limo felt so wrong. We were riding in style while our daughter was dead. What sense did that make?

All of our relatives and Shannon's closest friends gathered in the youth room of the church. There were at least three or four dozen people. I remember Barbara saying, "For being an only child, I sure have a lot of relatives!" That bit of humor helped lighten the moment. Shannon would have liked that.

As two o'clock approached, we went into the sanctuary. I remember glancing at the congregation as we walked in. The church was *full*! And the flowers! There were more than sixty bouquets on the platform. I'd never seen so many flowers. Later, Barbara felt sad that I hadn't been able to read the notes individually and enjoy them more. Instead, I'd had to content myself with glancing quickly at what had been written.

The participants

Shannon had appreciated women pastors, so we wanted to have a woman give the homily. We asked Julie Scott to do it, and she was the perfect choice. Although Julie isn't a minister, she is a very spiritual person. I had officiated at her marriage to Kraig Scott. Shannon was ten years old at the time, and she had been very impressed with the young couple. Later, Julie had taught Shannon and had been one of her mentors. Now, at Shannon's funeral, Julie gave a poignant, comforting, and especially meaningful homily.

Karen Johnson, vice president for development at the college and another of Shannon's mentors, read the life sketch, and Dr. Loren Dickinson, longtime family friend and a professor of Shannon's, presented the eulogy. Henning Guldhammer and John Brunt participated by offering the prayers; Peggy and Charles Bell played a flute and English horn duet; Kraig Scott played a wonderful arrangement of " 'Tis So Sweet to Trust in Jesus" that he had written for the funeral. And at the conclusion of the service, Gary Tetz and Jim Hannum presented a video tribute they had made from home movies. Everyone who participated did so with compassion and grace.

The funeral service was everything that we had wanted, and it proceeded without a hitch, so I was able to relax.

It is the custom in our part of the world for those who attend a funeral to file by the open casket on their way out. The line of people at the funeral that Friday afternoon seemed endless. Shannon's family and close friends were sitting in the front rows of the church, and many, many of those in line stepped over to give us a hug or to shake our hands as they waited to pass by the casket. Barbara and I hadn't intended to greet people at that time, but eventually we stood up to receive their condolences.

At last it was our turn to say our final good-byes to Shannon. Oh, how hard it was to watch when the casket lid was closed for the last time. As we slowly made our way out of the church, Kraig played a piece that used a set of chimes that the graduating class of 1995—Shannon's class—had given to the college as their class gift. For me, that was a very meaningful touch.

Barbara and I had asked Jennifer Quast and a couple of other friends to have a part in the graveside service following the funeral. Jen had been Shannon's soul mate and treasured friend. She and Shannon had been excited that Shannon was moving back west because that meant that they'd be able to see each other more often. Now that possibility was gone.

The graveside service didn't take long, but it was very significant for us. Afterward, many people wanted to speak to us, while others were trying to hurry us off to the funeral dinner prepared for us and the out-of-town guests. We wanted to stay till Shannon was lowered into the ground and her casket covered with dirt, but we were told that many of the people who had come to the graveside service wouldn't leave until we did, and Barbara didn't want everyone present when the casket was lowered to its resting place. Leaving Shannon in that hole in the ground while we drove away to eat a meal made us feel as if our hearts would literally break.

At the dinner, we had the opportunity to talk with many people who had known Shannon and with many of Shannon's friends. During that time, we heard stories from college days that we probably never would have heard if the church hadn't provided that meal. For many people, it was a time of remembering and healing. Our very sociable daughter would have loved it.

Memorial service in Maryland

The Silver Spring church that Shannon had attended coordinated a memorial service for her. Pastors and members thoughtfully shared memories, addressed questions of why God would allow such a tragedy (see chapter 5), and reminded us of Scripture's promises of a better future.

This service provided the opportunity for family and friends in the Washington, D.C., area to support one another and express their care for us. They did so admirably. To hear from church members how Shannon's participation in their services had benefited them was a blessing. She was active in their youth group, in their program of providing hot meals for the homeless, and in their social activities. She enjoyed such things and participated enthusiastically.

Several people from the Chief of Navy Chaplain's office attended this memorial service, including the chief of chaplains himself. As a Navy Reserve chaplain, I had become acquainted with some of the chaplains through working with them on various projects, and I had met others in their offices. At the memorial service, their white summer uniforms stood out like light in a dark world.

Several of the chaplains stayed after the service and waited in a long line to express their condolences in person. Solidarity with those in uniform—those with

GOD'S VOLUNTEER

Shannon Marie Bigger

June 11, 1971–June 16, 1996

FRIEND TO ALL

LIVE FOR SOMETHING. DO GOOD. AND LEAVE BEHIND YOU A MONUMENT OF VIRTUE THAT THE STORMS OF TIME CAN NEVER DESTROY. WRITE YOUR NAME IN KINDNESS, LOVE, AND MERCY ON THE HEARTS OF THOSE YOU COME IN CONTACT WITH YEAR AFTER YEAR AND YOU WILL NEVER BE FORGOTTEN. YOUR NAME AND YOUR GOOD DEEDS WILL SHINE AS THE STARS OF HEAVEN.
—THOMAS CHALMERS

Our lives are forever changed—we miss you, Shannon!

whom I'd had the privilege to serve—was a great comfort. Shocked that they would come, I felt like a guest who had become part of the family. It brought a sense of relief and belonging that helped brace us against the onslaught of isolation.

A related expression of warmth came in the form of memorial contributions from Navy Chapel groups such as the one in Guam with whom I had worshiped. To think that people of many different faiths were united by our military service and religious faith cheered us. Those contributions, along with many others, jump-started an endowment fund for student missions that bears Shannon's name. Those funds, along with the funds that continue to come in, provide financial support for students who volunteer a year of their lives to teach in classrooms on the Micronesian island of Yap.

Shannon's gravestone bears a profound challenge given by Thomas Chalmers, a Scottish preacher who ministered during the nineteenth century. This challenge speaks of the commitment to service epitomized by both military service members and student volunteers.

> Live for something. Do good, and leave behind you a monument of virtue that the storm of time can never destroy. Write your name, in kindness, love, and mercy, on the hearts of thousands you come in contact with year by year: you will never be forgotten. No! your name, your deeds, will be as legible on the hearts you leave behind you as the stars on the brow of evening. Good deeds will shine as the stars of heaven.

CHAPTER THREE

The Media

Our tragic story was big news in the Walla Walla Valley. We were asked to meet with the media from the local Tri-Cities (Richland, Pasco, and Kennewick) TV stations. As we drove up College Avenue to meet the crew, we noticed that the flag in front of the administration building was at half-mast. Seeing that honor paid to our daughter was wonderfully sad for us. What a tribute! But it did make the reality seem more final somehow. The campus seemed very subdued during the time between spring graduation and summer school. People seemed to talk in hushed tones, although in reality, I don't think I really heard anyone talking. Just a perception I had.

It had been big news in Washington, D.C., too. Reporters there had pounced on the story of Shannon's murder, arriving at the apartment building with TV cameras soon enough to broadcast Shannon's being carried out of her apartment in a body bag. It was a wrenching visual image—one that played over and over in our minds as well as on the TV screens all around us. It was unbelievable that our precious girl was inside that big plastic pouch! It seemed that the D.C. TV stations played that scene over and over—so much so that acquaintances began to phone us, horrified and wishing to commiserate with us.

The Maryland police, the staff at the state's attorney's office, and several friends encouraged us to be skeptical of what we heard on the news. They promised to keep us fully informed as to what they learned, and they kept that promise in every way, which was a great comfort to us.

They also warned us to avoid media contact, reminding us how invasive media questions can be. They encouraged us to decline interview requests, yet we were also struck with how our tragedy might be a way of reaching out to others who had experienced similar losses but felt isolated or ignored. So, contrary to the prevailing wisdom of many of the law enforcement and legal professionals who were working with us, we decided to make ourselves available to reporters. Our campus public relations people—Stephen Payne, Rosa Jimenez, and Joanne Reinke—consulted with us. Stephen even used his own frequent flier miles to be with us in Washington, D.C. He was an invaluable asset.

We asked cousins Don and Linda to do us the favor of recording the news stories and sending them to us. Rather than hardening us to the trauma Shannon suffered, this connection with the place where she lived and died helped us feel more in touch with it. But some of the reports frustrated us.

As human beings, we are prone to finish in our minds the things that we see around us that are only partially clear. When we see someone drive a car behind a building, we're prone to wait and watch till we see it emerge on the other side. If we see a line that disappears behind a foreground object, we're likely to look for it to appear on the other side.

Composers, arrangers, and other musicians make use of the auditory form of the same phenomenon. When they write or play two or three notes of a chord, our mind fills in the missing tones. If we hear several notes from a familiar tune, we will complete the phrase or song in our mind.

Reporters do something similar. They try to fit the pieces of a story together. Consciously or unconsciously, they work to create a story line that makes sense, that describes the events they record, that explains the unseen and previously un-known. As with putting a puzzle together, they fit things together piece by piece until a picture begins to emerge. Keen observation, good questions, and sound reasoning lead them to appropriate conclusions and identify them as outstanding reporters.

But when people make assumptions, when they tinker with experiences that don't seem to fit the present situation, when they conjure details that point to the ending they expect, when prejudices and hunches become suggestions and then conclusions, the picture they paint clouds rather than clarifies.

One story line we found painful was the suggestion that Shannon was a naïve country bumpkin who had been swallowed up by the big city. Moving from a quiet little Western town to the big city was just too complicated for her. She wasn't prepared to live safely in this setting. Like a deer on the highway, she was in the wrong place at the wrong time doing the wrong thing—and was smacked by the dangers that lurk in those surroundings.

The evidence found in the first few hours after Shannon was found dead led them down that path. Her door was found ajar, and it bore no sign of forced entry. Did that mean she let Anthony into her apartment? Did it mean she left the door unlocked? Was she too careless and/or too trusting? Would she still be alive if she had been more careful, more street smart?

To us, these questions sounded like those who asked them were making excuses for the crime. They were justifying a murder because they thought it wouldn't have happened had she been more savvy. They implied that Shannon herself was at least partially responsible for her own death. That made her twice a victim.

But we knew that Shannon was careful. When we first visited her in Maryland, she instructed us on what we must do to be safe there. Don't open the apartment door unless you know who's knocking on the door or ringing the bell. Walk wide around the corners of buildings. When you're walking, cross the street to avoid potentially dangerous situations. Look in the back seat of your car before you get in. Carry your keys in your hand so you can get in easily and quickly, and once inside, lock your door immediately.

Shannon was *very* careful to follow these rules herself. Several weeks before her death, her uncle came to visit her. He arrived at her apartment before she returned from work, so he decided to take a walk. When he returned, he saw that her car was now in the lot. He went to her door and knocked, but there was no sign that anyone was inside the apartment. He knocked several more times and still got no answer, so he turned to leave. As he did so, Shannon opened the door. She said that before he moved, she hadn't been able to see him through the peephole—that's why she hadn't opened the door right away.

Soon after that incident, Barbara spent some time visiting Shannon. The refrigerator in Shannon's apartment wasn't working at the time, so the manager called a repairman. Barbara was staying in the apartment while Shannon worked, so Barbara agreed to let the repairman in. When Shannon got home after work, she chastized Barbara for opening the door without asking who it was, and then she phoned the office to verify that the repairman was legitimate.

So I repeat: Shannon was cautious!

The media's suggestion that we hadn't prepared Shannon to survive outside a small, safe community intensified the pain and guilt we felt because we weren't with her when she needed us most. Parents are supposed to protect their children. It's our responsibility to launch them safely and well prepared into a sometimes hostile world. Our physical separation was already a huge burden for us. Now this implication that we had somehow failed to prepare her adequately for her immersion into the adult world added to our pain.

Barbara felt that especially keenly. She was the one who had traveled east with Shannon when Shannon moved. They drove Shannon's car and pulled a small U-Haul trailer with all her belongings in it.

On that trip, the two of them had enjoyed a wonderful time together. After attending an extended family reunion in western Montana over the Fourth of July, they headed to Maryland. They visited Mount Rushmore and the famous Wall Drug in South Dakota and sang along with Disney CDs for hours.

When they arrived in D.C., Barbara and Shannon looked at several of the potential living locations that friends and relatives had suggested, as well as some they discovered. They chose the one they did because of its safety record, its single entrance, and its twenty-four-hour-a-day surveillance camera. Besides, this apartment had the black-and-white kitchen floor that Shannon had seen in a dream. It seemed to be the right place. After Shannon's murder, Barbara was haunted with second-guessing her support of this choice. We already were guilt prone, and the suggestion that we could have done more to help Shannon live safely intensified our burden.

That said, by and large, the media were very thoughtful. They asked whether we were willing to visit with them. They also asked permission to be at her memorial service. And they let us share whatever we wished to share and didn't badger us for additional information.

CHAPTER FOUR

Shannon Was . . .

Who was this Shannon—this young woman whom we lost? We have vivid personal memories and family stories from our life with her. But Barbara and I were deeply touched as we heard other people describe her and as we learned how they perceived her.

The life sketch Karen Johnson read at Shannon's funeral pointed out that Shannon was a people person who was active in ministry.* And the people who contributed to the eulogy that Dr. Loren Dickinson presented described her as a person "who delighted in the world of ideas, who was energized in the presence of others, who was serious about making something significant of her life," and who wanted God to be at the center of her life. Those who knew her described her as kind, gentle, thoughtful, sensitive, perceptive, sweet, and as a believer. They said she was a caring person who valued fairness and justice, but they also noted that she was always upbeat and was a good listener who was dependable and who had a sense of humor.

We seldom have the privilege of hearing people describe us or the people we love in that way. We take those in our lives so much for granted that we don't reflect on what impresses us about them—let alone share those reflections with them. Artists look for the qualities people have, and so do writers and musicians. But too many of the rest of us get so caught up in our activities that we omit reflecting on the people who are important to us. We are so intensely involved

---

* You'll find both the life sketch and the eulogy that were read at Shannon's funeral in the appendix at the back of this book.

with other people that we spend too little time paying attention to the people who really count in our lives, appreciating the little things they do and say, and acknowledging how they influence us.

But when they're gone, we think about such things. Peak emotional experiences then become our norm. We find ourselves there whether or not we've chosen to be there. We're forced by the circumstance of loss to recognize the value of others and in what ways they will be missed. Grief pushes us to the core issues of humanity, such as how much we love some people and dislike others, and such as how the absence of little things that we've seldom, if ever, noticed creates an aching void. In that context, let me share some of our reflections about Shannon.

Upon our return to Oregon from the seminary, we had been assigned to pastor three churches that served a swath of cowboy and logging country several hundred miles long. We lived in Burns, Oregon, the year that Shannon was born. A sleepy town supported by surrounding cattle ranches, loggers, and a lumber mill, its small hospital had no ob-gyn specialists. But the staff members were kind and personable, and they shared our excitement about the birth of our first child. At birth, Shannon weighed eight pounds, ten ounces. She was a big baby—which stood in sharp contrast to the slenderness that was characteristic of her for the rest of her life.

When Shannon was two years old, we moved from that rural environment to southern California so I could attend postgraduate school. Shannon adjusted to the change in her world at least as easily as Barbara and I did. A year after we moved, Hilary was born. That important marker was followed by my completion of my graduate studies. Rather than moving back to Oregon, we continued to live in California for several more years. The girls thrived in their metropolitan life, and they were happy to call California home. When, years later, we moved to Walla Walla, Washington, a small town in the Northwest, they experienced frequent bouts of homesickness and loneliness for the bigger city.

Shannon was thin and dainty as a child, but her appearance didn't match her personality. She was confident in front of a congregation and enjoyed being a member of a leadership group—though one on one, she was much shyer than many would have guessed given her public persona.

Responsible to a fault, her academic achievements were based more on her consistent focus on what needed to be done than on any big flashes of insight or inspiration. Shannon made decisions based on her convictions and her long-term goals. We could count on her being true to herself.

Not one for confrontations, she preferred to walk away from an uncomfortable situation rather than to work at changing it. This isn't to say that she never was combative. She just chose her opponents very carefully. At times she made life miserable for her little sister; but as they grew older, Shannon backed away from confrontations with Hilary—even those she could have won by claiming the privileges of her age or her seniority.

Shannon hit her stride in college. There, she found others who shared her values and interests at a level she hadn't experienced before. She became part of a circle of friends who enthusiastically supported one another—a positive, optimistic, Christian circle of friends. They devoted themselves to helping others and to encouraging and inspiring one another.

During her sophomore year, Shannon was determined to go somewhere overseas as a volunteer. In those days, many Walla Walla College students were going to Palau. But while Shannon wanted a warm climate, she didn't want to be surrounded by people she already knew, so she chose to go to an island named Ebeye instead. However, when she told her friend Brian Klokeid what she was planning, he said, "Let me tell you about Yap." And after that, Yap it was!

So, Shannon chose to spend a year in voluntary service as a grade school teacher on that small island in the Pacific. That speck of land had a powerful influence on her. She grew up there. She overcame adversity there, saw miracles happen there, fell in love with the children there, and was loved there. Shannon became independent there—a capable young woman who had learned to communicate with God and who was confident of her place in His kingdom.

When Shannon came home from Yap, she seemed more settled, more mature and purposeful than she had been before her time on that island. She opted out of two romantic relationships and focused instead on her friends, her studies, and her pending career. Inspired by her teachers to use what she was learning to raise money for good causes, she was selected by Washington Adventist Hospital to do a postgraduation internship in their development office. The year she spent there was a challenge in many ways, but she was excited by the experience.

Shannon had never lived in the eastern part of the United States. But Barbara's cousin Linda Steinert and her family lived in Maryland, where Shannon was going, and they provided her with a family connection while she explored the East. She had a grand opportunity to venture into the political center of this nation, to explore our historical roots, and to experience the working world.

She also joined a local congregation, where she thrived and felt spiritually nurtured and affirmed. Pastors Dan George and Patrick Williams were filled with grace and insight, and they immersed Shannon and other young adults in work for others. Their youth groups did the usual recreational outings and trips, but they also periodically joined other church members to work at a soup kitchen that served homeless people.

Shannon spent time with church friends and family visiting sites in the Capitol area, attending events on the National Mall, strolling through the Smithsonian museums, walking along the waterways and canals, and wandering through the national arboretum and wildlife areas.

Several times during that year my Navy Reserve assignments took me to the Chief of Navy Chaplains office in Washington, D.C. On those occasions, I stayed with Shannon and cherished the opportunity I had of seeing her live as an independent adult away from her childhood home and family. No longer our little girl, she was independent now, able to function on her own; capable of structuring her own life, generating stable friendships, and making the most of a challenging work setting.

She enjoyed the excitement of being near D.C., but the end of her internship year brought a job offer from Gem State Academy, a Christian high school in Idaho. Her on-site visit and interview for the position of director of development and alumni communications went extremely well. She felt that she resonated with both the staff and the students, and she was very excited about joining them.

We also were very excited. Now Shannon would be much closer to home, much closer to us. I was to drive to Maryland in early July, load her things into a trailer, and caravan west with her.

Just two weeks before that day, the horrible news came . . .

CHAPTER FIVE

Where Was God?

A friend wrote the following to me:

This world is tainted by Adam's transgression. Add to that a mix of motives and necessary free will, and for millennia you have a seething cauldron of competing spiritual realities. Enter Jesus. The atonement made real spiritual progress possible—but not inevitable. Free will can and does lead many into darkness, while others choose the Light of the World as their refuge. The battle continues—even escalates—as we draw nearer to the end of time. God's Kingdom comes, where His will is done. Where the enemy's will is paramount, lives are lost forever, and untold human suffering runs rampant.

In desperate times many find solace in the eye of the whirlwind—a place of sanctuary where deep wounds are cauterized by the fire of God's love. I have ventured into the abyss and battled for my life more times than I care to remember. In the darkness I have been exposed, broken, but also empowered. Where I have died, He all the more lives in me. That is the way of sorrows so easily shunned for more pleasant climes.

You have walked a bitter road and seen what evil unrestrained can do, and you have persevered even in the depths of sorrow and despair. Your reward, dear friend, is more of Him and less of you—that place where eternal life penetrates the humdrum existence of the masses and moves heaven's understanding tears to flow. He is present. He is love—pure and unending love. He bears and shares your pain. He is your Savior, and your Sanctuary.

You are greatly loved, my brother.

V/R Alan

So e-mailed my friend Alan Kieran. He echoed thoughts voiced by Patrick Williams, one of the pastors who officiated at Shannon's Takoma Park memorial service.

Where was God when Shannon was killed? He was crying as He did at the grave of His friend Lazarus. Crying deep, loud, agonizing sobs that sounded like thunder and shook the ground on which He stood as an earthquake would have shaken it.

Where is God when we suffer? Crying and mourning and grieving with us.

But in our hour of desperation, even that seems insufficient. We want a tangible God, a visible God, a God who acts—a God who interrupts the forces of evil and prevents the pain that brings us sorrow. Where is such a God when we need Him?

These questions haunt all who look to God for refuge when they suffer. Barbara and I, along with our friends and family, asked these questions in many ways. As we watched the TV image of Shannon being carried down the stairs from her apartment in a body bag, these questions echoed in our minds. Through our sobs and tears, these were the questions that troubled us. As we looked at each other with hollow eyes, these were the questions that mattered. Sometimes we even spoke them aloud. Where was God when Shannon needed Him? Where was God when she was stabbed and slashed to death? The quest for answers led through these questions.

Uncertainty haunted us. We wanted to *know*—not just to question. We wanted to understand, to find explanations for what had happened.

We aren't alone. All on whom the tragedies of the world fall walk this path in one way or another. We assume that explanations will bring comfort. Like a little child whose knee is scraped or whose head is banged by a fall on the playground and who then runs to Mommy or Daddy, we may turn to God for reassurance. When we ache with concern for someone who cries out in pain, we, like our granddaughter, turn toward the stable people we know and ask, "What happened?" Comfort and explanations are important to us.

But danger lurks in our search for answers. Explanations feed misplaced optimism. For example, political campaigns spout promises to solve society's ills. But we learn the hard way that after the elections, despite their promises and plans, politicians cannot solve all our problems. Scientific discoveries raise our hopes for cures to the ravages of disease. But scientists cannot save us. In fact, supposed explanations sometimes distance us from real answers by masking the real problems. These explanations merely address the symptoms, not the root causes of human woes. They point toward the false gods of science or government or technology. They send us scurrying to human strongholds and tempt us to trust our sufficiency. But all of that is a delusion.

The ancients looked to pagan idols and mythological beings for help. Remember Psalm 121:1, 2?

> I lift up my eyes to the hills—
>   where does my help come from?
> My help comes from the LORD,
>   the Maker of heaven and earth.

Remember the faulty advice of supposed friends that the besieged look to a mountain hideaway for protection?

> In the LORD I take refuge.
>   How then can you say to me:
>   "Flee like a bird to your mountain.
> For look, the wicked bend their bows;
>   they set their arrows against the strings
> to shoot from the shadows
>   at the upright in heart.
> When the foundations are being destroyed,
>   what can the righteous do?" (Psalm 11:1–3).

No easy answer

We kid ourselves if we pretend that we can find easy answers. Many profound thinkers, including many believers, have struggled to find good explanations for the existence of evil. Survivors of much more catastrophic massacres than Barbara and I experienced have thought and written about how they cope. Historians and philosophers ruminate about causes and lay out what they think went wrong. While those efforts are important and can point us toward some helpful suggestions, none ultimately has the magic solution that satisfies everyone.

The truth is that this world is an evil place. Bad things frequently happen here—many times without provocation. Innocent people suffer. Better to let the reality of evil sink in than to pretend it doesn't exist or that we can cure all that causes it. Having been warned centuries ago, we Christians expect evil to surround us.

> We wrestle not against flesh and blood, but against principalities, against powers, against the rulers of the darkness of this world, against spiritual wickedness in high places (Ephesians 6:12, KJV).

Barbara and I have found comfort in a paradox—a limited application of a fundamental truth about Christianity: acknowledging the overwhelming power of evil points the way to overcoming it. Jesus acted out that truth in His incarnation. By becoming human like us, Jesus has lifted us above our human limitations. By submitting to the ravages of sin, Jesus overcame sin. By submitting to the cross, which was intended to impose a humiliating defeat, Jesus gained a stunning victory.

We have found comfort in surrendering to truth—the truth that this world is an evil place. The truth that horrible things happen here. The truth that life isn't always fair or just. The truth that we are helpless to change what has happened. The discovery of our helplessness leads us to admit that we desperately need a Savior. Anything short of that, and we'd be at risk of trying to solve our own problems, of relying on human wisdom, strength, and skill to lift our race from our condition.

Easy solutions and quick answers hide the ultimate answer from us. But when we admit our helplessness, when we let ourselves be overwhelmed, we see our desperate state. Abraham Lincoln once wrote, "I have been driven many times to my knees by the overwhelming conviction *that I had nowhere else to go.*"

Desperation turns us to God, and in God we find hope!

Praise be to the God and Father of our Lord Jesus Christ! In his great mercy he has given us new birth into a living hope through the resurrection of Jesus Christ from the dead, and into an inheritance that can never perish, spoil or fade—kept in heaven for you (1 Peter 1:3, 4).

Then I saw "a new heaven and a new earth," for the first heaven and the first earth had passed away, and there was no longer any sea. I saw the Holy City, the new Jerusalem, coming down out of heaven from God, prepared as a bride beautifully dressed for her husband. And I heard a loud voice from the throne saying, "Look! God's dwelling place is now among the people, and he will dwell with them. They will be his people, and God himself will be with them and be their God. He will wipe every tear from their eyes. There will be no more death or mourning or crying or pain, for the old order of things has passed away" (Revelation 21:1–4).

Promises such as these are wonderful harbingers of the distant future, but our hope for the future should change our lives now. Because we hope to live forever, we ought to be easier to live with now. Because we have hope for an eternal future, we ought to be more optimistic now. Because what we believe about the future changes our attitude in the present, we ought to be happy now.

This is not to suggest that we cope best with the present by escaping to the future. We accept the present, face reality, and let ourselves be overwhelmed by it. That is no escape, no retreat from the rigors and horrors of life now. In fact, we combat our present pain by facing it.

Embracing the pain

I have found it helpful to return to the city, the neighborhood, and the apartment complex where Shannon was killed. I drive into that entry, park in her parking lot, and frequently even walk up the stairs to what was once her door. By doing so, I embrace my pain—and prevent it from terrorizing me. To avoid that place would isolate me from that part of my past, and many of the memories I have of our daughter are there. If I were to separate my life today from the evil that happened there, evil would win. Not only would it have taken her, but it would also have taken from me that place full of my memories of her. No, we don't want to avoid the present by escaping to the future. But our hope for the future gives us a framework on which we can build a sustainable present in the face of tragedy.

Years ago while I was in chaplain training at Loma Linda University Medical Center, our supervisor, Charles Teel, acquainted me with a very helpful book. At the time I was assigned to the cancer unit, in which a young father was dying. His decline and inevitable, painful death disturbed me emotionally and spiritually. Why would God allow this to happen to a young man whose wife loved him, whose children adored him, and whose family relied on him for security and stability? Did God not care? Was He not able to intervene? It was in these circumstances that Chaplain Teel gave me a copy of *The Will of God*.

Written during World War II by British pastor Leslie Weatherhead, this book contains several of the sermons he preached to a congregation that was dwindling because its husbands, fathers, and sons were being killed. Like me, the grieving widows and orphans and friends were asking questions. They were wondering about God—how He could allow such heartbreak. How He could condone such travesty.

Weatherhead's approach, oversimplified here, was to remind his parishioners that God originally intended something quite different. God's "intentional will" was to have a perfect world where peace and productivity and happiness flourished. But God honors human freedom above all else. He won't impose Himself or His ways on unwilling people. While God intended that human freedom would always be exercised for the good of others, His commitment to it means He must allow people to make destructive choices.

Since God chose that option, He promised the first humans that eventually He would replace the tragic present with a future perfection. His "ultimate will" would mirror His "intentional will." In the meantime, God stays within the limits of the option He has chosen. In order to preserve human freedom and allow each individual to choose her or his own ultimate destiny, God cannot end evil. He doesn't create it, mind you. But when the consequences follow as the natural result of the choices people have made, He usually allows them to stand. God's "circumstantial will" allows the natural order of things to function as the default mode. Only occasionally does He intervene miraculously, and then He usually does so for reasons we don't understand adequately. In the meantime God gives us hope. He promises to walk with us through the dark times of our lives.

In the aftermath of Shannon's death, Karin Thompson, one of Shannon's schoolmates since grade school, reminded us that Psalm 23, so often used as a comforting funeral text, doesn't promise life without problems. It only promises that God will accompany us even if that means going through the valley of the shadow of death with us. God promises to be with us in our dark days. When we are threatened and terrified by evil, God takes away our fear. "Yea, though I walk through the valley of the shadow of death, I will fear no evil, for You are with me" (Psalm 23:4, NKJV).

How can we pray to a God who allows such painful suffering? And if we do pray, what do we say to a God who most often chooses not to intervene supernaturally in the usual flow of human events?

Kris, the man Hilary married, articulated a profoundly helpful focus for our prayers. Instead of praying for escape and deliverance, he suggested we should pray for wisdom to make good choices, courage to do what we know to be right, and comfort that will enable us to endure the bad things that happen to us. We have found that a very helpful way to connect with a God we still believe to be capable, caring, and interested in us.

> Who will separate us from the love of Christ? Will hardship, or distress, or persecution, or famine, or nakedness, or peril, or sword? . . . No, in all these things we are more than conquerors through him who loved us. For I am convinced that neither death, nor life, nor angels, nor rulers, nor things present, nor things to come, nor powers, nor height, nor depth, nor anything else in all creation, will be able to separate us from the love of God in Christ Jesus our Lord (Romans 8:35, 37–39, NRSV).

God assures us that our present suffering has meaning. Our struggles are significant and in the end will produce something worthwhile. "We know that all things work together for good for those who love God, who are called according to his purpose" (verse 28, NRSV).

Our hope

We also believe that God is stronger than evil. The result of these battles between good and evil is already determined. Memories of a powerful sermon that I heard years before Shannon was killed buoyed me. The preacher, who had lost a child in a motorcycle accident, had based his message on the book of Revelation. He drew from that book its portrayal of our struggles and then presented the promises that God made to counter those struggles. The preacher said,

> The book of Revelation describes the trials of the churches, the opening of the seals, and the suffering of the saints. But I have been to the end of the book!
>
> Revelation describes the souls crying under the altar and the woman chased into the wilderness. But I have been to the end of the book!
>
> Revelation describes the seven last plagues, but I have been to the end of the book!
>
> I have read about the victory of the Lamb, the fall of Babylon, and the marriage supper of the Lamb. I have read about the New Jerusalem coming down from God out of heaven, about Satan's defeat and the creation of a new heaven and a new earth. I have been to the end of the book!

Yes, we face evil in this world, but we are not defeated by it. We have been to the end of the book!

We suffer and mourn and grieve. But we have been to the end of the book!

We let our helplessness overwhelm us, but we know the victory story of the Lamb of God who takes away the sin of the world. We have been to the end of the book!

> Brothers and sisters, we do not want you to be uninformed about those who sleep in death, so that you do not grieve like the rest of mankind, who have no hope. For we believe that Jesus died and rose again, and so we believe that God will bring with Jesus those who have fallen asleep in him. According to the Lord's

word, we tell you that we who are still alive, who are left until the coming of the Lord, will certainly not precede those who have fallen asleep. For the Lord himself will come down from heaven, with a loud command, with the voice of the archangel and with the trumpet call of God, and the dead in Christ will rise first. After that, we who are still alive and are left will be caught up together with them in the clouds to meet the Lord in the air. And so we will be with the Lord forever. Therefore encourage one another with these words (1 Thessalonians 4:13–18).

We find hope not by avoiding pain but by embracing it, by recognizing in it God's promise of something better. Even while we're still in the desert, we catch glimpses of the Promised Land.

Remember the story of Moses' disappointment? Raised in the fertile Nile delta, he fled to the desert for forty years and then returned to Egypt to take the Israelites to the land of promise. After forty years of wandering in that desert, they approached the place they had dreamed of for so long. But God forbade Moses to cross into that land with the people he had led for all those years. Instead, God led him up Mount Nebo. Poised on the edge of the desert sand, the brown, barren mountain range juts up from the desert floor. From its peaks, one can see to the east the desolate sands of the desert and to the west the fertile valley of the Jordan River. God led Moses to a place that gave him a view to the west so that he could see what was to come for God's people.

When Shannon was killed, Doug Clark, who chaired Walla Walla College's theology department and who was an archaeologist by profession, was in Jordan. He sent an e-mail one Sabbath to tell us that he hadn't gone to church that day. "Instead," he said, "in memory of Shannon, I climbed Mount Nebo to look again at the Promised Land."

One answer

Of course, Barbara, too, has struggled with God's apparent absence when we or someone we love needs His protection. Here's her perspective on this question.

Where was God on that Father's Day? That question plagues many of Shannon's family members and friends. I have a vivid picture of one thing He was doing that day. As the life of our precious daughter was ending, He was gently cradling her in His arms and rendering her unconscious to what was happening to her.

Despite this horrific event, I can't be angry at the God whom Shannon loved with all her heart. All the hope I have rests in Him.

Shannon's deep, abiding love of God was an encouragement to many, including me. She often felt ostracized because of her faith. Yet though she felt very lonely at times, she had every confidence that Jesus really was her Best Friend. And she lived that conviction.

No, I'm not angry at God; but I do have a deep hatred for Satan and what he has done to us, to our family, to Shannon's host of friends, and to the myriads of people who would have benefited from knowing her. I almost feel guilty for hating him so much. But then I remember that he was so evil that he had to be cast out of heaven.

Hilary, too, has encouraged me. Like her, I want everyone—including the devil—to know that no matter what he tries to do to me, my love for and hope in Jesus is strong and secure. I *will* see Shannon again, and all the questions I have won't really matter then.

No, I'm not angry at God. He gave us a precious gift for twenty-five years and five days. He allowed us to nurture her and to be blessed by her. But it's true that I don't understand why He chose not to intervene in the time of terror that Shannon suffered. Maybe it's because He knew she was ready to meet Him. Whatever His reasons, He's making good come out of her tragic death.

God has been with me in a variety of ways. He has "put skin on Himself" and ministered to me—and to us—through hundreds and hundreds and hundreds of letters, cards, phone calls, and e-mail messages from all over the world. People who don't even know us have called or written to say they're praying for us. I know that has sustained us day by day.

God also uses people's arms and voices. Before Shannon's death I wasn't a touchy-feely person, but since then I have hugged literally thousands of people—and that's been good. People talking about Shannon, sharing memories of her, and just crying with me—all of this has been helpful. Don't ever think you shouldn't mention her to us because thinking of her will be too painful for us. The pain is always there anyway, and talking about her brings a measure of healing.

Through a rather miraculous set of circumstances, my parents were able to move near us, too, and on a June 11—Shannon's birthday. We can now look back and say that God made this move possible because He knew we'd need each other. I'm an only child, and having my immediate family nearby has been a tremendous blessing.

I have learned that the influence we have is much broader than we realize. We're still learning about how widespread Shannon's influence was. People from all over the world—many of them former Walla Walla College students—have written to tell us about the impact Shannon had on them. I know she'd be amazed to hear their stories.

One person wrote to us: "Shannon was a friend to me when no one else was." Another said, "As you well know, Shannon will never be forgotten." Others have commented: "I remember her cheerful attitude, sense of humor and *terrific* school spirit." "We will all miss Shannon deeply. I already miss her encouragement and friendship." "Shannon was our R.A. for the first year we were students at WWC. We do not know how, but she managed to be there for every single one of us when we needed her."

A grade school classmate said, "Her bright smile and ever upbeat attitude are a big part of the memories I have of my school days—Shannon touched my life, and how special a friend she was to me while we were growing up." And a former neighbor wrote, "I had the opportunity to get to know Shannon on a plane flight when she was returning from her teaching assignment in Yap. We had a good visit. She truly loved people, and I could tell [that] her teaching experience was very rewarding. Shannon will be missed by everyone who knew her."

Shannon was known for writing notes of encouragement to young and old. She was still keeping in touch with her Yapese students on their birthdays and at Christmas. Even when she was discouraged, she thought of others and tried to brighten their day. That's why I have confidence that I will see her in heaven. She lived her faith simply, but with the Blessed Hope always before her.

CHAPTER SIX

Hope in Spite of Evil

Barbara and I aren't the only people who have more than enough reason to wonder where God is when we need Him. In those parts of the world where there's a "thanksgiving" on the calendar, people face that question annually—and on many, many occasions between those holidays as well.

In our country, it was the Pilgrims who inaugurated the first Thanksgiving. They appreciated the food they had garnered in the first harvest in their new home. Their treaty with the Native Americans in the area was holding, and the fifty-three European colonists were joined by some ninety of their neighbors for a three-day feast.

This event is often romanticized in grade school. The students color and cut out pictures of pumpkins, Pilgrims, turkeys, and corn. They make hats like those the Pilgrims wore and act in plays picturing happy Pilgrims and Native Americans eating comfortably together. But the reality is that those long-ago days were not nearly so happy and comfortable.

The Pilgrims had landed the previous December 21. Winter had already set in, so most of them stayed on board their ship, the *Mayflower,* while a working party constructed shelters on shore. They were dangerously short of food. Scurvy, malnutrition, pneumonia, hypothermia, and frostbite took their toll. By the time autumn had arrived, only 53 of the original 102 Pilgrims—including only 4 of the 18 adult women who made that journey—survived to eat the first Thanksgiving meal.

Give thanks? Whatever.

My father-in-law used that expression, "whatever," on me. A radio feature about what this century and its first decade should be called intrigued me, so I told him about it. I began with questions: What is another name for the nineteenth century? (The eighteen hundreds.) The twentieth century? (The nineteen hundreds.) So, should we call the twenty-first century the twenty hundreds?*

And what about the decades? What were the 1950s nicknamed? (The fifties.) The 1960s? (The sixties.) The 1970s? (The seventies.), and so on. So what do we call the first decade of the century we're in—"the zeros," or "the ciphers," or "the double zeros," or "the aughts"?

Now, Dad is more serious than some of the rest of us are. He reads the newspaper from front to back, and he fills his days with books about history and with biographies of important people. So, tired of my frivolous questions, he just said, "Whatever!"

Whatever. That word used to indicate a kind, gentle deference to another person, as in "whatever you'd like." It meant you would happily do whatever that person chose. Now, it's either a genuine expression of disinterest, of uninvolved abandonment, of giving up, of distancing oneself from impending decisions, or it's the top-of-the-heap, passive-aggressive brushoff that replaces phrases such as "Forget that!" and "Not on your life!" and "In your dreams!" In the latter case, it's a milder form of several more direct and confrontational expletives and of obscene gestures that we would never use.

Give thanks? Whatever.

You have friends and family who are experiencing difficult challenges. They may be reeling from devastation caused by natural disasters, or suffering the consequences of accidents, or struggling with depression because of their poor choices, or burdened with watching the suffering of loved ones who have terminal illnesses, or grieving the loss of ones they loved.

Give thanks? Whatever. How can we give thanks when there is so much sadness?

Suffering and celebration

Scripture says, "Praise the LORD . . . and forget not all his benefits" (Psalm 103:2). If you lost your job, would that be your thought?

---

* In case you're wondering, the preferred answer is the aughts.

"Give thanks to the LORD, for he is good" (Psalm 106:1). If you were confined to your home by age or disability, would you say the Lord is good?

"I will sing the LORD's praise, for he has been good to me" (Psalm 13:6). If you were in a wheelchair today, you would say God has been good to you?

When I served as a Navy chaplain, I had orders that sent me to New Orleans many times. During those times I frequently worshiped at an African American church there. I appreciated their use of a call-and-response greeting—when they met, one would say, "God is good," and the other would respond, "All the time!"

Years later I went back to New Orleans to attend a convention that was being held there. I tried to phone the African American church I had attended years before, but a recording announced, "The number you have dialed is no longer in service." So I rented a car and drove to the church.

The neighborhood looked about the same as it had when I had been there before, and the church was still standing. But someone had spray-painted a "Do Not Enter" symbol on the entry, and when I peered through the windows, it was clear to me that the church wasn't being used.

I walked across the street, rang the doorbell on a house there, and asked the man who responded about the church. He said it had been severely damaged by Hurricane Katrina and was no longer in use. Then I asked him if his own house had been damaged. "Oh, yes," he said. They'd had to do a lot of work on it before they could live in it again.

If I had greeted that man by saying, "God is good," could he have honestly replied, "All the time"?

"Praise be to the LORD, for he has heard my cry for mercy" (Psalm 28:6). Years after Shannon taught on the island of Yap, another young woman, Kirsten Wolcott, served as a volunteer schoolteacher there. She, too, was murdered, and her family received her body on Thanksgiving Day. Would you say God heard that family's cry for mercy?

"Give thanks to the LORD, for he is good; his love endures forever" (Psalm 107:1). Those words are repeated four more times in the Psalms. If you had buried your wife or mother, would you believe that description of God?

Jill Lamberton, a classmate of Shannon's, sent us the following poem. Written by Edna St. Vincent Millay, it seems more appropriate at times of loss than does the exuberant gratitude of the psalmists.

I am not resigned to the shutting away of loving hearts in the hard ground.
So it is, and so it will be, for so it has been, time out of mind:
Into the darkness they go, the wise and the lovely. Crowned
With lilies and with laurel they go; but I am not resigned.

Lovers and thinkers, into the earth with you.
Be one with the dull, the indiscriminate dust.
A fragment of what you felt, of what you knew,
A formula, a phrase remains,—but the best is lost.

The answers quick and keen, the honest look, the laughter, the love,—
They are gone. They have gone to feed the roses. Elegant and curled
Is the blossom. Fragrant is the blossom. I know. But I do not approve.
More precious was the light in your eyes than all the roses in the world.

Down, down, down into the darkness of the grave
Gently they go, the beautiful, the tender, the kind;
Quietly they go, the intelligent, the witty, the brave.
I know. But I do not approve. And I am not resigned.
    (Edna St. Vincent Millay, "Dirge Without Music")

Give thanks? Whatever.

The biblical prophet Habakkuk knew those questions. Like the author of the book of Job, Habakkuk writes about an apparently absent God, an indifferent God who does nothing to protect His followers or control the wicked. Disaster and suffering are the lot of the loyal, perpetrated by agents of evil. Where is God?

Habakkuk's Complaint
How long, LORD, must I call for help,
    but you do not listen?
Or cry out to you, "Violence!"
    but you do not save?
Why do you make me look at injustice?
    Why do you tolerate wrongdoing?
Destruction and violence are before me;

there is strife, and conflict abounds.
Therefore the law is paralyzed,
    and justice never prevails.
The wicked hem in the righteous,
    so that justice is perverted (Habakkuk 1:2–4).

The Babylonians lurked at the borders of Israel as Habakkuk wrote. Israel couldn't protect itself from the impending invasion and the subsequent consequences, which would devastate the social and religious integrity of the Israelites. The present was dire; the future grim. Habakkuk and his people needed help! What a discouraging prospect!

Why complain?

We know those times and circumstances, don't we? We know what it means to feel helpless and hopeless. We know what it's like to be overwhelmed and stressed out. We understand those who throw up their hands and give up. We know.

No wonder, then, that many would rather smile and ignore the truth than face it. They would rather pretend that bad things have not happened to them and hope the memories and questions will go away.

But Habakkuk and other Bible writers show us another way. That way begins with our complaining to God. I've found that complaining to God brings several benefits.

First, complaining kept me—and keeps me—engaged with God. Complainants encounter God when He seems to be absent or silent, and that connection, even though negative at the time, is the first step toward regaining confidence in God.

Many psalms begin with a forceful confrontation of God, challenging Him to do something, to respond, to take care of us. After making those initial complaints, the psalmists almost always reach a resolution—an understanding of God's presence and a renewed confidence in His protection.

Have you heard it said that the opposite of love is not hate but indifference? As long as conflict exists between people, it at least shows that they want something from the other and that the connection matters to them—the relationship matters to them.

Elie Wiesel, the Holocaust survivor to whom the following saying is often attributed, talked of his struggle with God. He said, "I have not lost faith in God. I have moments of anger and protest. Sometimes I've been closer to him for that reason."

Second, complaining expresses hope. When we're unhappy with God and saying so, we're showing that we want something better. We would soon tire of complaining if we thought there was no chance that it would be effective. Our complaints to God imply that we believe He exists and that He can do something to fix our problem.

To stop complaining is to give in to suffering and loss. It says that we don't believe that God does cares or that He can or will intervene. Complaining to God expresses confidence in Him.

Finally, complaining leads to new insights. When our experience contradicts our beliefs, something has to change. For example, if we believe that God is powerful and kind, but we experience watching a loved one suffer through months of pain and then dying an agonizing death, we have a problem. It seems that the only alternatives are that either God is not kind, as we had believed He was, or He is not powerful enough to prevent this kind of suffering. Our experience seems to deny our beliefs.

It seems, then, that we must give up either our beliefs or our experience. What a dilemma! If we sacrifice our beliefs and trust only our experience, we lose our faith in God. On the other hand, if we ignore our experience but maintain our beliefs, we distance ourselves from reality and retreat into a fantasy world. Either alternative leads to an unbalanced, unhappy life.

In his book *Risking Truth: Reshaping the World Through Prayers of Lament,* Scott Ellington points out that this crisis of faith actually offers an opportunity for growth. The apparent impasse can become the catalyst to a new level of spiritual understanding and relationship with God.

These confrontations between experience and belief are scary for most of us. They threaten our stability and launch us into new territory. They call us to find new ways to explain God's character or to make peace with the mysteries we do not understand.

God's answer

Now back to Habakkuk. In the remainder of chapter 1 and on into chapter 2, God responds to Habakkuk's plea. He answers, explaining why the situation is as it is, and He describes what He intends to do about it. As a result of confronting God, Habakkuk's turmoil finds a response. His relationship with God is preserved.

The story God told Habakkuk was not all pretty. Bad news was part of God's message. In the short term, there would be significant distress for the Israelites. But in the long run, God's plan would prevail.

Remember the statement Jesus made to the disciples centuries later? They were worried about being left alone, abandoned by Jesus, their Leader. But He said to them,

> "Very truly I tell you, you will weep and mourn while the world rejoices. You will grieve, but your grief will turn to joy. A woman giving birth to a child has pain because her time has come; but when her baby is born she forgets the anguish because of her joy that a child is born into the world. So with you: Now is your time of grief, but I will see you again and you will rejoice, and no one will take away your joy. . . .
>
> ". . . A time is coming and in fact has come when you will be scattered, each to your own home. You will leave me all alone. Yet I am not alone, for my Father is with me. I have told you these things, so that in me you may have peace. In this world you will have trouble. But take heart! I have overcome the world" (John 16:20, 21, 32, 33).

Habakkuk suggested something similar. In light of the discouraging present, he looked for a better future—an ultimate, final, and permanent solution to the consequences of evil. He didn't abandon his faith because of human tragedy. Nor did he deny the evil and suffering around him. He believed in God's care in spite of the reality of what was happening.

Chapter 3 of his book records his response to God. It begins as follows:

> LORD, I have heard of your fame;

I stand in awe of your deeds, Lord.
Repeat them in our day,
in our time make them known;
in wrath remember mercy (Habakkuk 3:2).

The rest of Habakkuk's prayer in chapter 3 reminds the prophet and his audience of how God acted in the past. By recounting that history, Habakkuk and his readers are reminded that God hears, God cares, and that God does, in fact, act. By rehearsing that history, Habakkuk recovers confidence that God hears and cares *now*, in spite of experiences that seem to contradict that belief.

What Habakkuk says anticipates the theme of John's Revelation. John prophesies trouble and tragedy, but he remains optimistic. Why? Because he knows how the story ends!

In John's book of Revelation, we read about the trials of the churches—but we have been to the end of the book!

We hear about the opening of the seals and intense human suffering—but we have been to the end of the book!

We read about the woman chased into wilderness—but we have been to the end of the book!

We read about the seven last plagues—but we have been to the end of the book!

At the end of the book we read about Satan's defeat and the fall of Babylon. We read about God's victory and the marriage of the Lamb. We're told about a new heaven and new earth.

Give thanks? Oh, yes!

Habakkuk also anticipates a similar expression by the apostle Paul, who encouraged complaining to God about our hardships as a means to renewed relationship: "Don't worry about anything; instead, pray about everything. Tell God what you need, and thank him for all he has done. Then you will experience God's peace, which exceeds anything we can understand. His peace will guard your hearts and minds as you live in Christ Jesus" (Philippians 4:6, 7, NLT).

Give thanks? Absolutely!

CHAPTER SEVEN

Grief and Pain

My family and I aren't the only people who have experienced trauma. Nor is the trauma we've suffered the worst anyone has ever suffered. Compared to the Holocaust, what we have experienced is insignificant—just a relatively small illustration of the horrific results of separating human beings from God.

We have friends who were in Rwanda during the genocide there, and we grieve with those who suffered such huge losses. As a Navy couple, we stood on the tarmac at Dover Air Force Base with the families of sailors who were killed in the attack on the USS *Cole,* and I've had the assignment of telling the families of Navy and Marine service members killed in Iraq that their sons would be coming home in caskets. I have even officiated at the funerals of several of those service members. So my family and I don't pretend to have a corner on sudden tragic loss.

What do people of faith do in the face of death? We can't sit back and say, "It's OK." It's *not* OK. And we can't pretend that death is something to be taken lightly, as if it has no consequences. The truth is that it devastates us. As Edna St. Vincent Millay so poignantly expressed in her poem "Dirge Without Music" (see chapter 6), while death is inevitable and to be expected, we mustn't become complacent about it. God has instilled in us a longing for eternal life. We should protest anything short of that.

In our grieving we've tried to figure out what happened in Shannon's apartment when she was murdered. You might think that's a waste of time because Shannon and Anthony were the only witnesses, and Shannon's voice has been silenced and Anthony has told so many stories that it's impossible to know which one—if any—is true. Though there's no way we can know with certainty what really happened, we have been able to discount several of the early suggestions. For instance, we know that Shannon was very careful, so we reject the idea that she got in danger's way because she was naïve and too trusting. We are convinced that she didn't know Anthony and that she didn't welcome him, a stranger, into her apartment. Nor would her lifestyle invite this sort of violent attack: she didn't use drugs, hang out with violent people, frequent bars, or pick up guys.

What then is the real story?

Some possibilities bring a bit of comfort. Under severe stress, Shannon had a tendency to freeze emotionally and even to "lose it" at times. It's possible that when she realized the danger she was facing, she fainted and thus didn't know what Anthony was doing to her. And in fact, the detectives have suggested that she may have been "rendered unconscious very early" because there was no sign of a struggle either in her bedroom or on her body. We're very grateful for that.

The sinister reality

People are tempted to say, or at least to think, "If only she had lived someplace else," or "if only she hadn't been so naïve," or "if only she hadn't been so trusting," or "if only Anthony's poverty hadn't pushed him into despair and hopelessness," or "if only we could solve the problem of . . . ," and on and on and on it goes. We reject the idea that Anthony's attack on Shannon was prompted by poverty or mental illness or his race or any personal or societal problem. Anthony was not just one individual gone bad. He was an example of the much more sinister reality that evil permeates every human being.

The idea that we can eradicate evils like Shannon's murder by solving societal or personal problems suggests that we can save ourselves. But this isn't rational. No one can make sense of a senseless world. The rush to quick and easy explanations creates false expectations and short-circuits our search for the real problem and the real solution. Barbara and I don't look to politicians or social service agencies or police departments to prevent violence. These individuals and agencies can control it to a degree, and we need to do what we can to keep society as safe and constructive and productive as possible. But our efforts can do little to stop the tide of evil—and it is evil that is the problem. Anthony's attack on Shannon was just one example of what Satan's disastrous influence in our world is producing. We can't end the evil that's destroying our earth and those who live upon it. Only God can. He has promised to do so at the end of this age—a promise made certain by the victorious life, death, and resurrection of Jesus. Anything short of that ultimate solution fails to solve the problem.

Initially, the murder of Shannon didn't fill me so much with anger as it did with overwhelming feelings of sadness and loss.* Plunging completely into these emotions without opposing or distracting feelings brought me a great deal of relief.

Sometimes anger provides a helpful counterbalance to sadness. Unending, unlimited sadness produces prolonged depression, and at the extreme can lead to suicide. That was never a concern for me because my sadness, though profound and sometimes overwhelming, never pushed me to that level of paralysis or suicide. Anger, the appropriate response to pain, can be just as destructive if it isn't tempered with sadness. Unending, unlimited anger can lead to violence, and in the extreme, to murder.

My childhood struggles with anger had made me worry that if anyone ever were to attack a member of my family, it would take several big, strong people to prevent me from fighting back. Initially, God shielded me from those instinctive reactions. The sense of sadness mixed with peace I felt at our time of crisis wasn't the result of my own study or choice or willpower. It was God's gift.

So, Barbara and I have had the blessing of being able to leave the "why?" questions unanswered. We don't know why. All we know is that this is an evil world, and because we know no more than that, we have been pushed to our knees by the overwhelming realization that we have nowhere else to go.

Gifts of comfort

In the middle of our loss we received many comforting gifts. I've mentioned already the presence and support of friends and family, the cards and letters and calls, the neighbors and fellow workers who surrounded us with emotional comfort and practical help in those early days. Gardeners planted flowers in our front yard. Animal lovers fed our horses. Pastors shared nods and sadness and Scripture. Cooks prepared meals, writers composed notes, and caregivers gave

---

* However, as Anthony responded to the legal process with defiance, the anger I felt became a serious problem. See chapter 8.

hugs. All were comforting. But none of this changed the reality that Shannon was dead. The thoughtful acts of kindness didn't solve the problem, although they did help us get through those difficult times.

Shannon's death also brought us a gift of meaning—meaning that came through words and songs and thoughts that many shared with us. Meaning from the look of peace and rest on Shannon's face as she lay in the casket. Meaning from the reminder of the story of Lazarus—a reminder that when God seemed absent, He was just getting ready to raise the dead.

We also have experienced the gift of time. As time has rolled on, the wrenching reality has become a memory. The images are not as vivid; the memories are more distant; and that's a relief.

We also have the gift of hope. Paul says it so well in his letter to the Thessalonians. In an evil world we don't escape grieving. We just grieve differently than do those who have no hope. Here's how Paul put it:

> We do not want you to be uninformed, brothers and sisters, about those who have died, so that you may not grieve as others do who have no hope. For since we believe that Jesus died and rose again, even so, through Jesus, God will bring with him those who have died. For this we declare to you by the word of the Lord, that we who are alive, who are left until the coming of the Lord, will by no means precede those who have died. For the Lord himself, with a cry of command, with the archangel's call and with the sound of God's trumpet, will descend from heaven, and the dead in Christ will rise first. Then we who are alive, who are left, will be caught up in the clouds together with them to meet the Lord in the air; and so we will be with the Lord forever (1 Thessalonians 4:13–17, NRSV).

"It is finished," Jesus said as He hung on the cross—not because all human suffering was finished, but because in God's eyes *what will be already is.* For Him, there is no distinction between the present and the future. Because He gained the victory on the cross, the ultimate conclusion is certain. We are hopeful because of God's promise to us that as we surrender ourselves to Him each day, the peace of God that passes all understanding will guard our hearts and minds in Christ Jesus (see Philippians

4:6, 7). We are hopeful because nothing can separate us from the love of God (see Romans 8:38, 39). We are hopeful because God's love is stronger than evil.

So we are humbled and awed that the gifts of friendship and time and meaning and hope have come to us. We are so grateful that we are able to trust in Christ, not because of our self-discipline or avid study, but because He chooses to give us that gift of faith.

Comments

My resentments—a flashback:

> I resist this notoriety. We're pushed into the spotlight for all the wrong reasons. Everywhere we go, we're greeted with condolences. I resent the reality of my life being defined by Shannon's death. Events are dated before or after her murder. "How are you doing?" means "How are you coping with your grief?" Barbara and Hilary tell me I'm aging before their eyes. I don't have the energy or creative excitement for life I used to have. I'm much more annoyingly compulsive, demanding, restless. I'm preoccupied with thoughts and feelings associated with Shannon. I have to remind myself to smile. Life now revolves around Shannon's death. It has become the reference point for my life. I *hate* that. Why should I live my life around a death? Why should all dates and feelings be tied to that one? Why should my life remind me of her death?

This preoccupation produces another hazard. So much attention to Shannon's death elevates that horror to a place of prime focus. When all our thoughts revolve around that event, it becomes the center of life and thought and memories. It makes her death the predominant fact of life, and, as such, it becomes an idol. Theologian Paul Tillich may not have had in mind such morbid objects of our attention when he described the danger of idolizing things, but our unrelenting attention to this event threatens very similar results.

Hilary wrote the following regarding how Shannon's death has affected her, and what adjustments she has made:

I was suddenly an only child, struggling to come to terms not just with my loss but with the reaction toward me from my family and community. Growing up as a pastor's daughter, I was used to having a whole church full of people [who] knew who I was. Suddenly, [I] felt that an entire community knew who I was and had an opinion about this loss. I had spent my entire childhood in the shadow of a well-known and beloved father, and now I felt that Shannon's murder would be another factor in my losing my own identity. I struggled with what I perceived as Shannon's "saintification"—people who looked at Shannon's life as a string of near-perfect deeds. What did this say about me, a polar opposite of my sister, with whom I had struggled our entire childhood? Her many irritating qualities were still fresh in my mind, and, although we had certainly grown closer as we were becoming adults, we weren't the "best friends" that most people expected to hear about.

And then there were my own selfish desires and insecurities that were becoming awkward and nearly impossible to maneuver. I had already been planning my wedding when Shannon died, and we had set on a date—which was now going to be the one-year anniversary of her death. I was the center of what I perceived as, quite literally, "pity parties"—bridal showers and receptions that were well attended, in my opinion, solely because of Shannon's death.

The ramifications of Shannon's death have been far-reaching for me. I had always envisioned myself as a mother but [now] questioned whether I wanted to bring children into this world. I had personally experienced the worst of our world and felt that I should spare others from that exposure, even if it meant depriving myself of the experience of a family. Ultimately, we decided that we did want to have children, and I have found my experiences with Shannon—both in life and in death—have formed how I interact with my children. On the downside, I am forever anticipating the worst in life: what will I do if my children die? I have found that this constant nagging thought causes unneeded worry and stress for me, but it also encourages me to live life to the fullest and enjoy every possible moment with my children, more than others in my position.

Seeking stability

For months I felt overwhelmed—at first by sadness and then by an emotionless void. Family, friends, university colleagues, and students seemed to understand. At least, they didn't confront me about my shift in emotional tone or complain about my lack of energy and enthusiasm. Part of my class load at the time included social work students who were learning how to relate to stressed-out clients. Their gentle inquiries and attentiveness about our journey became a living lab experience for them. Theories found illustration as they respectfully and empathically listened.

Barbara and I shared our journey in class discussions and speaking appointments and in many other ways. Being willing to "live out loud" much of our personal experience of loss seemed to encourage other people and to keep us up to date with ourselves. Preparing for these public presentations pushed us to reevaluate ourselves, reassess what we were experiencing, and reconnect with the key anchors that kept us stable. Talking about our grief kept our inner selves cleaned out, so to speak, and prevented us from burying or ignoring what had happened. That was good for the listeners and for us.

Through the fall and winter we seemed to do as well as one might expect. Changes required adjustments, of course. Barbara, who had always been the quieter of the two of us, became very talkative. For her, talking seemed to release pent-up emotional energy. At times, we joked with each other that she had become like Shannon, who at times chattered incessantly!

While Barbara became verbal, I lost the ability as well as the motivation to express myself in words. For both of us, this was a dramatic change—one that Hilary says still hasn't been completely reversed.

Statistics tracing what happens to couples who experience traumatic events sobered us. We've had friends whose relationship disintegrated under the stress of a serious accident or sudden financial loss or severe illness or handicap. Statistics about couples who lose a child by violence are even worse than these other traumatic events—some studies show that up to 80 percent of them divorce. We were determined that wouldn't happen to us. Our marriage commitment to each other was a crucial value, second only to our allegiance to God. But the trauma we were dealing with had brought about significant changes in the spouse with whom we had lived for thirty years, and if we were going to preserve our marriage, we would have to accommodate those changes.

I had to adapt myself to a woman who had changed significantly from the one I married. Before, she had been the quiet one. Now she talked and talked and talked. The woman who for years had waited patiently for me to quit visiting with friends after church now was often the last one to leave. And frequently now, she was the one who was ready to talk about her thoughts and feelings.

Before, words had come easily for me. Visiting with guests and members in the foyer had energized me. But the shock of Shannon's death knocked the words out of me. For months and months I had nothing to say. I avoided the foyer when church was over, exiting through a side door to avoid conversations. What I was experiencing overwhelmed my ability to describe it. My world had become nonverbal. So Barbara had to adjust to living with the somber, silent introvert who had replaced the outgoing optimist she had fallen in love with years before.

For a long time, I even avoided printed words. Books and articles—a teacher's lifeblood—didn't interest me. Instead, I found that music—primarily, instrumental music—and poetry, especially some of the psalms, sustained me. The emotional catharsis of those expressions gave me some relief, a kind of visceral validation that connected to my reality. Several organ pieces by Bach were particularly reassuring. Firm and predictable and played at an unwavering tempo, they reminded me of how unstoppable and immovable life really is when viewed from God's perspective.

Individual rhythms

It soon became clear that in our grieving and recovery, each of us—Barbara, Hilary, Rosemary, and I—had our own rhythm. We didn't all feel sad at the same time—or tired or energized or overwhelmed or anything else. At times each of us was more anxious to talk about his or her inner life or work or school than were the others. Sometimes, one of us wanted to talk about something, but the rest of us weren't up to listening just then. We were in a delicate dance that required unusually high levels of tolerance and acceptance.

For example, the first December after Shannon's murder, Hilary had gone through Shannon's cedar chest and taken out many of her ornaments and decorations. She and Barbara were sitting in the family room when I came home. Hilary started telling me a story, but partway through it Barbara began looking at some of the ornaments. I asked if they were Shannon's, and she said they were. It stunned me—shocked me—that she would be going through them with such apparent abandon. Then I realized that I had interrupted Hilary's story and asked her to continue telling it. With some obvious frustration she said, "No, the time has passed."

At that I bolted to the living room, where I sat and sobbed and sobbed, alone. The sight of Barbara sorting through Shannon's things as if that were routine made me sad. My inability to focus entirely on Hilary even for a short time made me sad. (How in the world could she compete with a dead sister?) And Hilary's hauntingly accurate comment, "the time has passed," made me sad.

Fortunately, we have learned to recognize and consciously accept the uniqueness of each person's experience. We stopped expecting others to feel what we felt and worked at supporting each other, even when what someone said he or she needed seemed strange to us. God has been good. We have learned a lot about each other and about ourselves—though, in my case at least, some of what I learned about myself wasn't pleasant.

Combining all of what we were learning and experiencing was—and is—no easy chore. It's hard to face the reality of evil without giving up hope. To invest energy and resources toward positive change while acknowledging that only God has the ultimate solution to evil requires delicate balancing. To accept gifts of friendship without becoming dependent, to be patient and allow time to aid healing, to recognize meaning in the context of painful disappointment, and to retain hope at times of chaos and loss—all of this challenges us. Surrender comes hard for independent and resourceful human beings. But to the degree that we surrender, we overcome. By trusting, we gain confidence.

While Shannon was on Yap, there was no church building, no pastor, no congregation. The church consisted of a few teachers and friends who gathered together to worship. Because they had no hymnal, for week after week they sang only summer camp choruses. Then someone found an old hymnal. Shannon got out her flute and played the song "'Tis So Sweet to Trust in Jesus." She said it reminded her of home.

Because of what that song meant to Shannon, it has become very special to us. It testifies of the blessings we receive when we surrender ourselves to God, trusting that He will see us through the valley of the shadow of death and that He will teach us to hope for a better future, for an eternal future even as we grieve.

'Tis so sweet to trust in Jesus,
Just to take Him at His word;
Just to rest upon His promise,
Just to know, "Thus saith the Lord."

Refrain
Jesus, Jesus, how I trust Him;
How I've proved Him o'er and o'er!
Jesus, Jesus, precious Jesus!
O for grace to trust Him more!

Yes, 'tis sweet to trust in Jesus,
Just from sin and self to cease;
Just from Jesus simply taking
Life, and rest, and joy, and peace.

I'm so glad I learned to trust Thee,
Precious Jesus, Savior, Friend;
And I know that Thou art with me,
Wilt be with me till the end.
(William J. Kirkpatrick, " 'Tis So Sweet to Trust in Jesus")

CHAPTER EIGHT

Release

When I was a child, my outbursts of anger were intense enough to cause concern, so I had to expend a lot of energy to control them. As I said earlier, I've always thought that if anyone tried to hurt a member of my family, my reaction would no doubt be quick and destructive. Fortunately, for months after Shannon's death God shielded me from my anger. That was a huge blessing.

Through the summer and fall after Shannon's murder, my sadness was so overwhelming that it completely obscured any hints of anger. The initial legal proceedings focused on gathering information and preserving it and on deciding what approach the prosecution would take, which depended on what Anthony would plead. The state's attorney, Robert Dean, and his office's victim witness advocate, Paula Slan, kept us up to date on the decisions the prosecutors were making.

Soon after Anthony's arrest, a preliminary hearing was held to take sworn testimony, particularly from the man driving the van on the day it was identified as the vehicle Anthony had used. Attorney Dean was anxious to preserve that testimony in case something should happen to the witness or he should move or disappear (an anticipation that became reality not long afterward). Hilary flew to Washington to attend the hearing. She was determined to keep herself completely informed about the case. Other family members joined her there, where they saw Anthony for the first time and heard some of the evidence that had led the prosecutor to file the formal charges against him.

Dean consulted with us about pursuing the death penalty. He said that option was viable and that our wishes would influence his decision about whether or not to pursue it. He then pointed out that capital punishment trials are almost always appealed, sometimes repeatedly, and they often drag on for years. And frequently in such trials the attorneys for the defense attempt to discredit or malign the victims so they can argue that the victims were responsible for precipitating the attack. They scrutinize the victims' lives and reputations, and they may misrepresent the victims or at least cast them in the worst light possible. We, as a family, discussed whether or not capital punishment is ever appropriate, and we came to differing conclusions. But no one insisted that we pursue that sentence in this case.

Growing frustration

Then something totally unrelated to Shannon's murder began to pile more stress on top of the load I was already carrying. Some people in our community were suspicious about the beliefs and practices of a group with which I was affiliated. They began to circulate wild stories about this group—stories that pictured everyone connected with that group as apostate.

I traced a couple of the stories back to their origins and found that both of them were false and were based on misunderstandings. The storytellers hadn't checked their "facts" with the people they were maligning, and other people were uncritically accepting their stories as true and passing them along without ever verifying them. Some of the people who were making these groundless accusations were people I had trusted, and that hurt me deeply.

Through that summer and fall my sadness deepened, and I experienced what depression does to people—wearing them down and sapping their energy, interest, and activity. I lost my appetite and felt discouraged and unhappy.

By that winter, flashes of energized aggravation were occasionally breaking through my depression. Barbara has always been uncomfortable with expressions of anger—even when it isn't directed at her. So my occasional venting alienated her, and the resulting increase of the distance between us added to my sense of isolation and intensified my frustrations.

Sentencing and appeals

On March 28—Good Friday—Anthony pleaded guilty to first-degree murder, to armed robbery, and to an Alford plea for attempted sexual offense in the first degree. In exchange for his guilty pleas, he was sentenced to life in prison without parole, plus life in prison, plus twenty years. We watched him all through the court session, looking for some sign of remorse, hoping for some word or statement of regret. There wasn't any. Anthony looked and acted detached, either unaware of or disinterested in the testimony given by law enforcement and mental health witnesses. Anthony's only reaction was a forceful obscene gesture that he made when the state's attorney concluded his presentation with a vigorous final statement.

When TV reporters asked our reactions to the sentences, I expressed regret. I said that two families had lost children—one by murder, and one by being locked up for the rest of his life. That was another very sad Good Friday.

Even before Anthony made that defiant gesture, I had given up hope of seeing or hearing anything positive from him. Now lingering questions, unfulfilled expectations, and the harsh reality and finality of it all seeped into me. My reaction was to feel more distance than animosity.

On April 21, a Monday, Paula Slan phoned, notifying us that Anthony had filed a request for permission to change his plea. She explained that in Maryland, this is the first step in the appeal process. She described it as a "leave to appeal" to the Court of Special Appeals. Because Anthony had pleaded guilty, he had to apply for permission to appeal. Attorney Dean tried to reassure us. He said it was almost certain that permission to appeal would be denied because as part of Anthony's plea bargain, he had waived the right to appeal.

The second appeal, filed at the same time as the first, was an application for review of his sentences. That request was sent to an administrative judge, who assigned three other judges to hear Anthony's appeals. These judges had the authority to change Anthony's sentence, but the only way they could change it was to decrease it, because the sentence he had received was the maximum that the law allowed. Attorney Dean warned that it might take several months before a court date would be available. And again, he said he didn't think we had any reason to worry.

Anger and rage

As the first anniversary of Shannon's murder approached, I began to feel my stress increasing and a deep reservoir of rage growing within me. Up to that time I had been so immersed in sadness and depression that Anthony's attempt to appeal his sentences hadn't bothered me. Even at the sentencing when I didn't hear or see any of the responses we hoped Anthony would make, I just sank deeper into detachment and emotional distance.

When determining what sentences should be imposed on those who have committed crimes, our legal system takes into account their state of mind and mental capacity. This helps the court determine what consequences the perpetrators should experience. So when Anthony appealed, wanting to change his plea to not guilty and to have his sentence reduced, the faint possibility that the court might actually respond positively to his request dramatically increased the load of anger I was carrying. The man who had admitted slashing and stabbing Shannon to death now wanted to escape the consequences of his deed. It seemed to me that any shortening of his sentence would suggest that his crime wasn't so bad after all—thus diminishing Shannon's loss, and ours.

But Anthony's unfortunate background and his consequent lack of abilities and options had triggered in me some feelings of empathy. That was troubling me now, because I feared that if I or anyone else acknowledged Anthony's poor start in life, one or another of the judges might be inclined to excuse his deed— or at least to reduce his sentence. Consequently, the anger that people probably had expected me to exhibit much sooner made its appearance now.

Before Shannon was murdered, I was healthy, my blood pressure was low, and I had no trouble relaxing or sleeping. Now, the knots in my stomach, the tension in my muscles, and the flashes of impatience alarmed me and made conversing with my students and preparing for the classes I was teaching very difficult.

Over the next several weeks, the reservoir of anger within me grew until it seemed large enough to consume me. I realized that unless I found a way to deal with my anger, it would destroy me, so I went to work.

For several years I had taught a class on stress management, so I knew the techniques well—deep breathing, progressive body relaxation, physical exercise, mental imaging, distraction, attitude changes, soft music. I tried to use them to reduce my pent-up emotions, but they didn't work.

The spiritual exercises that I practiced regularly didn't do the job either. I read the Bible and prayed, but the anger remained. I added biblical meditation and pulled up memories of times when God had brought healing to me, but these didn't alleviate my agony. Even my belief that God exists and that He is interested in our daily lives—truths I had accepted long before—didn't settle the matter.

Finding that my best efforts weren't helpful was discouraging enough, but the failure of my spiritual resources made me wonder what good they were. Could they provide any relief, any encouragement, when I was feeling such desperate need? Could they offer me any hope or any miraculous power? I struggled for weeks, searching for some way to reduce the emotional turmoil that was making me miserable.

Then, on a Sabbath that followed an especially intense week soon after the anniversary of Shannon's murder, I went to church feeling like an anxious, angry failure. What I heard in church that day made me feel even worse.

John Cress, the pastor who had informed Barbara and me about Shannon's murder, preached the sermon that day. He had stayed in touch with us and had been very supportive, but I hadn't shared my spiritual crisis with him, so he had no idea that I would zero in on one of the subpoints in his sermon, run off on a tangent, and be devastated by its impact.

John began by telling the story of Jesus' restoration of Peter after Peter had betrayed Him. Jesus asked Peter essentially the same question three times: Do you love Me? (see John 21:15–17). At that, my mind turned quickly to other things Jesus had said about love: "This is my command: Love each other" (John 15:17). "A new command I give you: Love one another. As I have loved you, so you must love one another" (John 13:34). It was when John read the next verse, "By this everyone will know that you are my disciples, if you love one another" (verse 35), that I went on a mental detour.

It was only a short step from those verses to others that pointed the finger directly at me: "You have heard that it was said, 'Love your neighbor and hate your enemy.' But I tell you: Love your enemies and pray for those who persecute you, that you may be children of your Father in heaven. He causes his sun to rise on the evil and the good, and sends rain on the righteous and the unrighteous. If you love those who love you, what reward will you get? Are not even the tax collectors doing that? And if you greet only your own people, what are you doing more than others? Do not even pagans do that?" (Matthew 5:43–47). "But to you who are listening I say: Love your enemies, do good to those who hate you" (Luke 6:27).

Oh no, I silently cried out, *not that! I've tried and tried for days and weeks and months. I've done everything I know what to do to love Anthony, and I can't make it happen. I, the lifelong Christian, the professional Christian, the Christian pastor and teacher, cannot do this one simple thing that You ask of me!* My failure to love Anthony led me to conclude that I was spiritually bankrupt and hopelessly lost because I couldn't represent my God by loving a fellow human being. I was devastated.

I had failed at other times in my life, so I knew well what it means to be embarrassed and deeply regretful. But this time the pain was much greater than it had ever been before. This wasn't just a minor matter—a hasty word or deed for which I was sorry. This time the failure came from deep within me. It involved the essence of who I am.

I knew Jesus wasn't calling me to forgive Anthony just one time. He was calling me to forgive Anthony at all times and for all time. My inability to do this revealed that I was faulty at my core. It meant that it wasn't just a matter of my needing to change my actions. I needed to change who I was too. But my identity ensured my failure; I knew that try as I might, I couldn't solve that problem. I couldn't change myself in that way. I was as much in need of God's transforming grace and as incapable of changing the reality of who I was as was Anthony in his cell in Maryland.

What a horrid thought that was—that spiritually, I was a peer of the man who murdered our daughter! That I was morally bankrupt and no better a representative of God than was a confessed murderer!

I felt crushed and farther from God than I had been at any other time in my life. Oh, even before Shannon was killed I could have made a long list of my shortcomings. I could have filled pages with examples of my mistakes and failures. There certainly were enough of them to separate me from God. This was far from the first time I'd had regrets. But there was something new and disturbing about what I saw of myself this time. The emotions surging up from my inner self were not prompted by some superficial annoyance. They weren't the result of a little slip, a small error on my part. They rose from the center of my being—the core of who I am. That day I saw myself as an angry, resentful, vengeful, cynical, destructive person.

For weeks, the anger and resentment I felt toward Anthony had been growing. I was connected to him, tied up with him, consumed by him. The man who had taken Shannon's life now threatened to take mine too—by so occupying my mind that he was becoming all I could think about.

Then I turned my attention to myself—and there I saw another very ugly picture. I realized that I, too, was a destructive person—a man of such limited spirituality that I couldn't stir up any redemptive feelings toward myself, let alone toward Anthony. I was incapable of doing what I wanted to do—unable to act in love toward myself or others. I was a wretched human failure, a man who needed God just as desperately as Anthony did. I was just as inhumane as he was, just as much a moral failure, just as incapable of being my best self. Both Anthony and I needed the same thing—the transformation that only God could give us. In that way I stood on a par with the man who had killed my daughter. What a humiliating discovery! While I was still in the church my mind screamed out, "O wretched man that I am! Who will deliver me from this body of death?" (Romans 7:24, NKJV).

Relief

The feeling of desperation lasted only a few seconds, but that was long enough for it to strip all pretense from me for a lifetime, if I permit it. No longer can I hide behind a façade of propriety, pretending to be a self-sufficient, God-fearing, people-loving person. Now I knew that on my own I can't do even the simplest moral good. Now I know that I, too, am a sinner in desperate need of a loving, saving God.

Once I had captured that picture and saved it as the home page in my mind, another text came to mind: "You see, at just the right time, when we were still powerless, Christ died for the ungodly. Very rarely will anyone die for a righteous person, though for a good person someone might possibly dare to die. But God demonstrates his own love for us in this: While we were still sinners, Christ died for us" (Romans 5:6–8).

Now *that* is good news! I'm a wretched man, but Christ loves me anyway! I'm a desperate failure who cannot cure himself, yet Christ died for me anyway. He didn't expect me to get things together and improve myself spiritually before He would help me. That profound reality warmed me. Never before had I felt like such a contented and happy failure! As the promise of God's forgiveness settled upon me, I could openly admit, without shame, that I was a sinner. When I realized this, feelings of relief filled me.

And then, suddenly, I noticed that the knot in my stomach was gone, I was no longer clenching my jaw, and I felt hungry and happy. Anthony was still on my mind, but resentment and anger no longer consumed me. The symptoms of stress that I'd been trying for weeks to jettison had disappeared in a matter of minutes.

The sermon over, we sang the closing hymn, received a benediction, and headed out of the church. As I walked up the aisle, I realized that not only was I no longer troubled with thoughts of Anthony, but the deep wound my former friends had dealt me no longer hurt. Even though I hadn't realized that the betrayal was partially responsible for the agony I had felt, the mistrust and pain that it brought had disappeared just as had my anger toward Anthony.

That experience changed my perception of forgiveness. I've come to understand it to be a gift, not a goal. I believe that the deep, profound forgiveness we all need comes from God. It isn't something we can obtain through self-help exercises and self-discipline. Our efforts to rid ourselves of the spiritual burdens we carry are useful and may relieve some of the stress and pain we suffer. But they don't address the fundamental pain that lies at the core of human distress— estrangement from God and failure to live up to His plan for us.

When we do face that central need and acknowledge our guilt, God bestows on us His gift of forgiveness. That gift, profoundly experienced, transforms us. It relieves us of our burdens and defuses our anger and resentment and desire for revenge. It allows us to give God our hurts and failures, and it fills us with the peace of God that transcends human understanding (see Philippians 4:7). And those who experience it can't help but share it with others.

CHAPTER NINE

Ten Years Later . . .

Ten years after Shannon's murder, Barbara and I were back in Washington, D.C. We had been there several times before. Business trips for the Navy as well as church and professional conventions brought us to that city. Each time we went there, we made ourselves drive into the parking lot of the apartment complex where Shannon had lived to look and remember. We were determined not to let the horror that originated there intimidate us into closing off any part of life, including that place. So we returned.

As we exited from the Beltway onto Georgia Avenue, my stomach began to tense up and my chest constricted. By the time we had reached Silver Spring, passed the turn to her church, and made the turn onto Blair Road, the discomfort was painful. I felt as though someone had punched me in the stomach. Breathing became a struggle, and I nearly pulled to the side of the road for fear that I would pass out. Grief was choking the life out of me, as it had during those first days after we heard that she had been killed.

When we turned into the parking lot by the apartment building, an empty space immediately in front of the stairway to her apartment waited for us. Almost always before, we'd had to drive around to the side of the building to find a parking spot. Why was this place open today? We were already sobbing, so we kept the car running with its air conditioner on to mask the sounds of our grief as well as to cool the humid summer air.

A mockingbird landed on the ground in front of us. As it hopped through the shrubs next to the building, it repeatedly stopped and looked at us—right straight at us, eye to eye. Was it mocking us, I wondered; making fun of our misery? No, I decided, not that. It was joining our sadness, speaking our language, sharing our pain.

Only at our first few visits to this place had the sadness been so heavy. Since then we'd made half a dozen trips there over more years than that without being paralyzed by the memories. Why again now, after so many years? For several days—in fact, even before we'd scheduled this trip to attend the retirement ceremony of our Chief of Navy Chaplains friend and former colleague Louis Iasiello—we'd felt the darkness building. The week before we'd left, I had begun to withdraw. Only after bubbling into tears while I was watching a TV segment that I normally wouldn't have considered emotionally touching did I realize what the date was—June 16, the date of the day on which Shannon was murdered.

Barbara had been especially teary, too, and she knew why. She had taught me how unchangeable dates are. "Yes," she would say, "we can give you your birthday presents on another day, but that doesn't make that day your birthday!" Convenience, preference, and emergencies notwithstanding, our celebrations had to take place on the days that the special events occurred or they didn't really count. That was true of the sad days as well as of the happy ones. We remembered the events that happened on the dates when they happened. Somehow our unconscious selves remembered exactly when that was.

In the 1960s Rod McKuen wrote the poem "The Gypsy Camp." It begins as follows:

> I put a seashell to my ear and it all comes back; the yellow sun
> . . . the Mediterranean blue, the sky, the children running on the
> beach that day, the killdeer birds marching in formation down to
> the sea, and back—when my memory wanders, as it does when
> bad things happen, I put a seashell to my ear and it all comes back;
> that day . . . you.

Every June, and sometimes in between, it all comes back to us. On that particular June day ten years after the deed, it returned with a vengeance. This time I didn't want to just sit in the parking lot and look; I wanted to walk up the steps, feel the stone slabs and grout under my feet, stare at her apartment door, imagine it standing ajar as it did the morning she was found, stand behind the pillars where Anthony may have lurked, and walk down the stairs to the laundry room and back up again to her landing.

As we sat there, a slender girl in her twenties carried bags of garbage to the dumpsters at the back of the parking lot. First one bag and then another and another tumbled into the bins. I wanted to shout to her, "Watch out! Don't relax! This is a dangerous place. Run back to your apartment and bolt the door!" But I was ten years too late, and time had silenced all but my tears.

Barbara didn't want to get out of the car. Being in this parking place was already too painful; she didn't want to get any closer. "I didn't see any security camera sign," she said. But it was there.

"Why did God lead us to this place?" Barbara asked, thinking aloud. "Everything seemed right. We thought it would be safe. Why would God do this to us?" She said Shannon had dreamed of an apartment with a black-and-white checkered kitchen floor. This apartment had a floor like that. Why had God let them believe this was the right place for Shannon?

Why?

* * * * *

The dogwoods have begun blossoming. A beautiful sight in all other ways, they hold a lot of memories. At Shannon's funeral, two families gave us dogwood trees. Other trees and shrubs and flowers followed. Today I notice the dogwoods in our town.

I notice them now because the ones at our house died. We finally gave up on them after trying several ways over several years to nurture them into health. They just wouldn't catch hold. One, especially, was weak. Each year it became more timid. More bark dried out and shriveled. More brown limb appeared between the clusters of leaves. Fewer and fewer leaves opened to the warm sunshine.

This sickliest of the three looked as if it had quit trying. The one we originally had did reasonably well. The one our local friends gave us looked as if it were doing OK, but it wasn't really hearty. The one given to us by my lifelong friends had the worst of it. Those friends suffered with us because they had lost a son and brother to cancer. It was as if, through the tree, they were suffering all over again. How we all wished that a vigorous and thriving tree would somehow bring back what both families had lost, denying the reality that linked us in grief.

The pine tree, on the other hand, finally took off. For years we had wondered whether it didn't like the West; if it were homesick for its native state and would never adjust to life here in the Northwest. The year after Shannon was killed, Barbara brought it home, carrying it on the airplane. She had attended a memorial service sponsored by the state of Maryland each year for families who had lost a member to murder. Those holding the service offered each family a pine seedling as a memento. Even though Barbara assumed the seedling wouldn't survive the several-day trip home, she brought it to show the rest of us.

The tree didn't look healthy when Barbara arrived, and we all assumed it was dead. But we decided to plant it and let our soil be its grave if it must die. We thought that like Shannon's grave, this spot might be the resting place of another life-form flown from Maryland and planted in the soil of the Walla Walla Valley. We wanted at least to try.

For several years, the pine looked stagnant. While the needles never turned completely brown, the shoot didn't seem to grow. A half dozen years after we planted the six-inch-tall seedling, it was still less than a foot tall. In spite of fertilizer, water, mulch, and careful attention to bugs and other parasites, it just didn't grow.

But then, a few years ago, everything changed. In a single year it added about three inches of new growth, with more than that the next year and even more the next. Now it stands nearly twenty feet tall, proud and green and gently swaying in the breezes of eastern Washington! It has become a welcome reminder of Shannon's first home of her own—a place she learned to love. It joins the other evergreens given by family and friends at the time of her death. All surround our yard with the majestic security articulated by Joyce Kilmer in his poem "Trees."

> I think that I shall never see
> A poem lovely as a tree.
>
> A tree whose hungry mouth is pressed
> Against the earth's sweet flowing breast;
>
> A tree that looks at God all day,
> And lifts her leafy arms to pray;
>
> A tree that may in summer wear
> A nest of robins in her hair;

Upon whose bosom snow has lain;
Who intimately lives with rain.

Poems are made by fools like me,
But only God can make a tree.

* * * * *

What did Shannon miss because her life was taken? She never knew the Naval Flag Class of 2000—eight of us Navy reservists who were promoted to the rank of rear admiral the same year. We became fast friends. We met two or three times a year. Often, we brought our wives, who became important members of our circle.

Our wives shared stories of how we each reacted to life, responded to challenges, pursued our ambitions, and related to our family and friends. The similarities were spooky! How could individuals from the diverse fields of business, education, aviation, architecture, and religion be so much the same? The Navy screening procedures had brought together a group who felt more like siblings or best friends than new acquaintances. We quickly became a band of brothers. But Shannon, who had been so proud of her chaplain dad, did not know them.

She didn't know Mark Hazara, who died unexpectedly when he was fifty-nine years old. He and some friends were on their annual camping trip. They had flown from Pennsylvania to Colorado and driven from the airport to the town that was their jumping-off place, unloaded their things, ate lunch, and boarded the gondola for the ride to the top of the mountain. Mark complained of indigestion, slumped over in the gondola, and was gone by the time he reached the top of the mountain. CPR was applied in the gondola and by EMTs at the top, but they couldn't save him.

Mark and his wife, Diane, had become close friends of ours. Even Kris and Hilary knew them and were saddened by his death. They remember Diane and Mark reaching out to them, including them in conversation, treating them like old friends.

Mark's death brought a double sadness for me in that it was our *surviving* daughter who knew and treasured these memories about him. All the years of getting acquainted and cementing our relationship with the Hazaras and the other flag classmates followed Shannon's death. We had moved on to the friendships and losses of a whole new group of people—and she wasn't part of it.

* * * * *

Today I'm flying home from San Diego, where I officiated at the wedding of David and Jenatte. This was another wedding that a cousin had invited me to conduct. David was several years younger than Shannon. In fact, ten years earlier, I had officiated at the wedding in which his older brother, Mike, married Caroline.

Shannon missed both of these weddings. Both were memorable events—high-energy guys who married optimistic and self-assured women. Two dentists who married two nurses.

Other siblings and cousins were there, parts of families with spouses and children. Shannon would have been among the celebrants with their exuberant smiles and quick-witted conversations. She would have loved seeing relatives and getting acquainted with those who were joining the family.

One of the last gatherings of this part of the extended family took place as she was heading east. We went to Yakima, where she enjoyed with us the fiftieth wedding anniversary of her great-aunt and great-uncle, Mike's and David's grandparents. The men's younger sister married later on. And their cousins married too, as did her sister Hilary, and Shannon missed it all.

* * * * *

A delightful addition to our life that also brought a measure of sadness was the births of our grandchildren. From the beginning our grandson was a cheerful, happy baby, and Kris and Hilary intentionally reinforced that. They laughed with him often, cheerfully solved his problems, and became the happy refuge where he could find comfort in his sad moments. Full of smiles, of energy for exploration and investigation, of delight at seeing friends and family, he was a wonderful, comforting gift to all of us. His aunt Shannon would have loved him.

As she had with her little students on Yap, she would have listened to his stories, would have made sense of the scattered tales, and would have interpreted his babbling. He would have felt accepted and respected by her and would have jumped up and down when he saw her, as he does with the rest of us. His aunt Shannon would have loved him, and he would have loved her—but they never met. How much richer would their lives had been if they had known each other? We'll never know.

Eagerly anticipated and excitedly welcomed, our granddaughter entered the world with a roomful of parents and grandparents anxious to love her. Would Shannon have been there? Would she have joyfully laughed and cried with the rest of us? Would she have seen how similar to her this niece was?

Barbara was the first to notice, or at least to acknowledge it out loud: the reddish-blond hair, the blue eyes, the very fair and heat-sensitive skin, the little button in the center of her upper lip, the slightest flat spot on her right ear, the quiet and passive engagement with life, protesting little and easily satisfied. Those things haunted Barbara. She felt as if she were holding Shannon in her arms again, reliving the memories of motherhood with her firstborn. But Shannon missed all of that.

How would Shannon, the talker, have related to her niece's turn of her head, her sidelong glances, and the demure roll of her shoulder? Would she have understood these nonverbal messages as well as she connected with the verbal ones?

And Rosemary's three children—what of them? Their quiet, lovable ways, raising their eyebrows in agreement with what is said and done, clearly connected to an island culture they've never seen. What stories and memories of Yap might Shannon have shared with them?

* * * * *

Jen has stayed in touch with us ever since Shannon's death. She and Shannon had been best friends, and losing Shannon was very hard on her. Rather than wilt away from those of us who reminded her of their friendship, Jen had opened herself to us. She introduced us to Greg while they were dating, asked Barbara to sit beside her mother at the wedding, invited me to participate with her pastor father in the wedding ceremony, and regularly shares e-mail news with us. She and Greg have extended the boundaries of their family to include us, and it has been good. We feel adopted by them, welcomed as "orphaned" parents.

An aside here: why is there no word meaning parents who have lost a child? We have words for those who lose a spouse and those who lose parents. But there is no name for a parent who loses a child. Their identity is confusing, lost in an intensified version of the vertigo childless couples must face when they are asked, "How many children do you have?"

Naming things gives us a sense of control over them and helps us understand them and the setting in which they live. Things that are unnamed exist in a shadowy uncertainty, a conundrum, a potentially threatening disruption to our sense of stability. This rootlessness is felt no less by the parents themselves than by those who meet them.

"How many children do you have?" There isn't a good answer. Strangers don't expect to hear a horror story any more than "orphaned" parents are anxious to overwhelm those who innocently introduced what they presumed would be a pleasant and positive connection with new acquaintances.

Back to Jen and Greg. Having a child didn't come easily for them. It required lots of both time and effort. But evenutally, after elaborate fertility studies and several attempts, they produced a successful pregnancy—and both of them and all of us in their cheering section were thrilled!

Wouldn't Shannon have loved to be part of that excitement? What would she have sent him as a baby gift? Would she have written notes to him and to his parents? What would she have said? Would she and Jen ever have gotten off the phone, or would they have continued sharing every impression and thought and idea forever and ever?

And would Shannon herself ever have married? What kind of person would she have married? Would they have had children? What mothering joys and sorrows, strengths and challenges, would she have known?

Shannon missed so much . . .

* * * * *

The woman's father was there first—there in the men's section of the store where I had come to exchange midcalf socks for an over-the-calf style. Later, her mother came. And then, while we were standing in the line to the cash register, she walked up, smiling, and said hello.

When I saw her, I was shocked. Not because she had arrived, but because she was beginning to look "mature." There were shadows and lines on her face.

Even though she was older than Shannon, they had seemed like peers to me. Now she stood there looking her age. (She must have been about forty.)

Would Shannon have been showing her age too? What would she have looked like? What would she have been through that would have put those shadows and wrinkles and other signs of life's hardships on her face? But Shannon isn't aging.

Instead, she's frozen in time, locked in her twenty-five-year-old youth, cemented in my memory as a young person.

How strange and sad is that?

* * * * *

Barbara and I were asked to make another trip to Micronesia. The tragic murder of Kirsten, a student missionary teacher, the previous month had created the need for grief counseling and support. Because of our professional training and our experience with losing Shannon, and because Shannon had also taught in that part of the world, they contacted us.

Even though Kirsten had been on the island only a short time, she had already made a very positive impact there, and she was loved. In some cultures, the names of the dead aren't written or spoken. But in spite of the hesitancy this cultural tradition created, a portion of the island road has been named for Kirsten. That touched us, as did visiting the impromptu memorial that stood where she was found.

The visit reminded me of the flowers, cards, and notes left after 9/11 on a slope near the Navy Annex. From that place one can see the place where the hijacked airplane crashed into the Pentagon. Mourners came there to remember the dead. That reminded me of my visit to New York City days after 9/11 and the Wall of Prayer on which were posted pictures, descriptions, and notes to and about hundreds of the missing and the dead.

For us, it has been comforting to hear Shannon's name. It reminds us that others remember her. It reassures us that she is not forgotten.

* * * * *

A man told us that Shannon had influenced a college student for good on the day of her funeral. This young person was not doing well—he was making poor choices and generally being irresponsible. He had missed a very important appointment with the man who was telling the story and then had showed up later, wanting to reschedule the appointment.

This man had been up all night working on a time-sensitive project, and he was exhausted. Upset that this student wanted to impose on him, he lashed out at the student, saying, "Over there in the church, a responsible young woman lies in a casket, while you have your life, but you're messing it up. You ought to be over there instead of her!"

Sometime later, that student told the storyteller that those strong words had changed his life. Shannon was indirectly involved in that student's new orientation, but she doesn't know the good her influence produced.

* * * * *

Shannon's death has made us keep an eye on life. We see its brevity, its uncertainty, and we take it more seriously now. Shannon has missed so much—but it's not just the dead who miss the good things of life. Too often the living don't see them either. So, in a way, Shannon's death has moved us to take a second look at life. In a way, it has given us a second chance to get from life all that we can.

Shannon's sister Hilary says, "Shannon and I were polar opposites as children, and growing up, I was nearly always irritated by most of her personality traits. But I have been given a second chance to appreciate and love her: I gave birth to her niece, who is exactly like her! My daughter not only looks much like Shannon, she acts much like her too. And I have realized that the constantly talking, wildly imaginative, overly affectionate, outgoing personality is a lot more fun than I remembered!"

And as for me, I'll conclude with these words: A second chance to appreciate and love—in what ways might I use that second chance to change how I relate to the irritating people and situations in my life? How might that opportunity change my perspective on the wounds and scars I carry? What paths to healing and hope can I trace with this second chance to look at life? Can I reclaim the value of Shannon's life by loving those in need of support?

So again, and finally, here's that Thomas Chalmers quotation that Shauna Gifford shared with us:

> Live for something. Do good, and leave behind you a monument of virtue that the storm of time can never destroy. Write your name in kindness, love, and mercy on the hearts of those you come in contact with year by year, and you will never be forgotten. No! Your name, your good deeds, will be as legible on the hearts you leave behind you as the stars on the brow of evening. Good deeds will shine as the stars of heaven.

PART TWO

Letting Go of Anger, Resentment, and the Desire for Revenge

CHAPTER TEN

The Context

Each of us has reasons to forgive. We've all been hurt, offended, betrayed, slighted, misunderstood, or misrepresented. We've experienced significant losses of one kind or another—the loss of a job, a friend, a spouse, a family member. The loss of hope for our advancement, or for the success of a project in which we had invested a lot of ourselves, or for the fulfillment of our dreams and expectations for our children or other loved ones. All of these disappointments and setbacks—slight or profound—raise the need to forgive.

Not only does forgiveness settle our emotional distress, but it also helps protect our physical health. And being emotionally and physically at ease enhances our relationships with others. So, since forgiving pays big dividends, the incentives to forgive are correspondingly large.

How does forgiveness work? How do we forgive? How can we become forgiving people? That's the focus of the section of this book that begins here.

It would please me to tell you that what follows is based on many years of study, research, thought, and analysis. The theoretical part of me—my left-brained, logical self—wishes that it had driven my investigation. But that isn't the case. What I've experienced preceded my understanding, and ongoing discoveries continue to surprise me.

That reality troubles me. Since by nature I base how I live primarily on reason, it bothers me not to have developed my theory of forgiveness before I needed to forgive. However, like the blind man whom Jesus healed, I could tell you what happened before I knew how and why it happened (see John 9:15).

It was the murder of my daughter Shannon—or, more specifically, her murderer's filing of appeals to be allowed to change his plea from guilty to not guilty and to have his sentence reduced—that stimulated my interest in the subject of forgiveness. During the years that have followed, I've tried to put a foundation of principles under what we know about forgiveness and how it works. There's a lot of good information available—information that in many cases can effectively alleviate the stress and burden that withholding forgiveness can generate. Understood clearly and put into practice with focused attention and effort, forgiveness can dissipate the grievances that sap our energy and spoil our happiness. By following the steps I discuss in what follows, we can improve our lives significantly.

But there are some offenses so grievous that despite the genuine efforts of those who have been hurt, they have found it almost impossible to forgive those who have hurt them. No two of us experience life the same way. What one person finds traumatic and long-lasting may to someone else seem like an insignificant bump in the road of life—one that can easily be leveled or driven over. No one can define for you how you should respond to what has happened to you.

The strength and depth of the rage that Shannon's murderer stirred up in me when he filed his appeal frightened me. And the struggle to let go of that rage left me feeling overwhelmed, helpless, and hopeless. I tried the approaches that had worked when I used them to deal with other frustrations I had experienced—good approaches, including some that I advocate in this book. But I couldn't shake the persistent poison of my anger and resentment.

Then, even though I felt that my efforts had failed and that God distanced Himself from me, He surprised me by rescuing me from myself. That dramatic experience transformed my attitude toward myself and toward those around me, including Shannon's killer. This didn't happen because of some choice I made or some accomplishment of mine. God took the initiative. He intervened. I was a passive recipient, gifted by the grace of God and puzzled by what had taken place. Unexpectedly, and unexplainably, my anger had disappeared. It was replaced by a peace that came without my choice or effort. It was this event, and my desire to learn how it worked that launched my inquiry. I wanted to understand what had happened to me. I wanted to comprehend rationally what had so dramatically changed my emotional state—had so truly transformed me.

Like a window

Feelings comprise a useful window on ourselves and our environment. They are the most personal revelation of our inner selves. Sharing them with someone else creates the highest level of intimacy attainable, creating much greater closeness than is possible when we restrict our sharing and discussing to ideas and facts. Sharing feelings—verbally, in conversations; or physically, in behavior (e.g., tone of voice, gestures, touch)—binds us more strongly to the one with whom we share than does just about anything else.

The person who hears and sees our spontaneous emotional responses to life and supports us rather than rejects us becomes part of our inner circle—an important colleague, a defender. Those who accept us because of—and especially in spite of—our feelings become intimate companions. This is why military personnel who share emotional experiences become a "band of brothers." This is why parents who endure a child's crying and temper tantrums melt with the child's hugs and smiles. This is why sex between two people is much more than just a physical act. This is why an agonizing journey of grief and rage and guilt and shame, capped by God's forgiveness, linked me so profoundly to God.

Touchy-feely experiences separated from reason worry me. I've thought and taught that because feelings are more spontaneous than rational, they comprise a poor foundation for decisions we make. While they may provide self-awareness, they don't give us the solid starting point, the life view, that is the foundation essential to understanding and acting logically. I've long encouraged students and counselees to require more than strong feelings when making decisions. Liking or not liking something is not an adequate basis for eating, buying, loving, marrying, punishing, or any other "ing"! To live one's life on the basis of feelings is to consign oneself to being blown in a different direction by every puff of wind that reaches us.

Feelings can be controlled, induced, chosen—and in that sense, understood. Our awareness of them allows us to figure out what prompted them and to decide how best to express them. But in my case, that process failed me. I had tried to choose peace and forgiveness, but I wasn't able to obtain them until I was confronted by the dark, sinister picture of who I really am. By providing that insight, God miraculously did for me what I couldn't do for myself.

How could God treat me so well? How could He possibly have been so gracious to me when He knew how spiteful, vengeful, cynical, and unforgiving I was? And how could what He did change my inner emotional reality so completely when I hadn't been able to change it on my own?

May these reflections on how forgiving works help you in your quest to become a forgiving person.

CHAPTER ELEVEN

Why Is It So Hard?

Writers have explored the subject of forgiveness for centuries. Many cultures have stories about people's willingness or hesitancy to release someone who has hurt them from their anger. And recent times are no exception—we still hear amazing stories about people who, instead of turning away from those who have hurt them—sometimes deeply—forgive the guilty.

We're reminded that holding grudges often creates high levels of stress, which, if not released, will eventually damage us physically, mentally, and spiritually. Living constantly in a state of sadness, anger, or hatred damages us. Headaches, backaches, jaw aches, and other, more serious physical ailments may grow out of some unforgiven grievance. Someone has said that refusing to forgive is like drinking a glass of poison and expecting your enemy to die. To preserve our health, we need to get over our grievances and get on with our life.

Refusal to forgive damages relationships too. When we are unhappy, angry, and hostile, we're unpleasant company. Often our frustrations with a perpetrator spill over onto people with whom we have no quarrel. In fact, sometimes the people we care about the most are the ones who suffer the most from our flashes of frustration. When we're with them, we relax, let down our guard, and let out our inner feelings. The people whom we trust to love us no matter what see us at our worst. We're not civil enough with them to screen our outbursts. As a wag put it, "Some people treat you like a member of the family, but most people have better manners than that."

Little doubt exists that we can learn to forgive. Numerous studies and reports have documented successful programs and have identified the attitudes and skills that we can use to become forgiving persons. Martin Doblmeier's documentary

The Power of Forgiveness chronicles several well-known incidents of tragic loss and contains interviews with people who intervened to bring stability, peace, and reconciliation, thus verifying that that we can learn to forgive.* Both religious and nonreligious people have found that they can move from anger to peace. And research conducted by my colleagues at Walla Walla University and me has shown that forgiveness training that has a spiritual component brings both short-term and long-term improvement. This kind of training lowers the level of hostility and enhances forgiveness.

Knowing the good that forgiveness does and that we can learn to be forgiving, why don't more of us do it? Why doesn't everyone forgive as soon as they're offended? Why not just do it and avoid all the damage that withholding forgiveness does to us?

Blocks to forgiving

There are four major reasons we withhold forgiveness. To obtain the benefits of forgiveness we must deal with all of them.

The first R, the first major reason we don't forgive, is that we are reluctant to face reality. Every incident that calls for forgiveness involves loss. We may have lost a limb, or a relationship, or our trust of someone with whom we had felt safe. All of these losses bring grief, and Elisabeth Kübler-Ross has said that our first response to grief is denial. We're tempted to ignore what has happened, to deny it, to go on living as if nothing had happened. Sometimes the truth that we have been hurt, abused, is just too overwhelming for us to face.

When a person whom I'll call Jim reached adulthood, he began to remember long-buried incidents that had happened in his childhood.[†] Jim's father was extremely harsh and demanding, and he flew into a rage whenever things didn't go his way. Jim's mother was of little help because she was timid, and she retreated whenever his father became upset.

---

* Among those interviewed are Virginia Commonwealth researcher Everett Worthington Jr., who is a pioneer in this field, and Fred Luskin, a prominent researcher known for his "Forgive for Good" program.

† To protect the identity of the people whose stories I've told in this book, I've deliberately blurred the details.

Jim was the first child in the family, so he caught the brunt of his father's anger. When he was a baby, his father wouldn't tolerate anything from him other than quiet cooing and smiles; fussing and crying would set him off, and he would begin to yell at baby Jim. As Jim grew older, his father added threats and blows, and sometimes he even threw him around.

Jim escaped his hurtful home life by creating a fantasy world to which he would retreat whenever his father got angry. He spent hours huddled in the darkness under the front steps of his house. And to further escape his horrible past, he buried the memories of his father's abuse beyond conscious recall. Not until he became an adult did he begin to recover the memories of his father's excruciating attacks. It was only when he admitted those memories to be true that he was able to put them aside.

If the trauma we suffered came later in life, we find other ways to avoid whatever or whoever has caused us pain. We may brush it off as unimportant or act as if it doesn't bother us. Or we may counterattack the perpetrator, or ignore him or her altogether. But burying our memories of being traumatized won't bring healing. Denial in any of its forms keeps us from dealing with our hurts, and it prevents us from forgiving those who hurt us. If we want our wounds to heal, we must acknowledge those wounds and deal with them.

The second R is regret. Have you met people who love to play the "poor me" game? They tell their sad story over and over again to people who have already heard it many times. And whenever anyone suggests a solution to their problem or offers healing for their hurt, they rush to tell more of their terrible plight. Locked in their grievance, they grovel in self-pity and moan continually about how terrible and unfair and unjust life has been to them.

Calvin Miller describes such a scene in his book *The Singer.* The book is a metaphor of the life of Christ, who is the Singer and who has come to offer new life to all who will choose it. In one story, the author pictures the Singer offering new life to a miller whose hand has been crushed by the huge stone at a gristmill. But the miller has become so fixated on his debilitating injury that even when the Singer promises to make the hand whole again, the miller remains focused on the past. He's so full of regret at what he's lost that he fails to see what the Singer is offering him, and eventually the Singer walks away, accepting the miller's unwillingness to be healed and leaving him in his misery.

I've noticed that I become energized when I resurrect an old offense and tell someone who hasn't heard the story of how it happened and the pain it's caused me. We get a dark comfort by holding on to our victim status, by seeking pity in which we can wallow, by taking the stage to relive an old hurt. When we've had weeks, or months, or years of practice, it feels normal to keep our old hurts alive. But doing so locks us into the past, preventing us from moving freely into the future. We become perpetual victims and give up the opportunity to try a different road.

We mustn't live in the past or find our greatest comfort in reciting our pains and regrets. Forgiving the offender enables us to close the door on the past and to take a new road, a new focus and purpose.

The third R word is rage—anger multiplied and out of control, or at least on the verge. The spectrum of this emotion ranges from irritation to annoyance to anger to rage.

People respond to injury by becoming either angry or sad. When a toddler grabs a toy out of another toddler's hands, the one who has lost the toy generally responds either by angrily grabbing it back or by sobbing as if life itself has been lost and all hope of recovery is gone.

Anger and sadness are opposite sides of the same coin—two ways in which we react to hurt or loss. They can be expressed independently or in combination with one another. Uncontrolled, they both lead to destruction: anger becomes rage, and if uncontrolled, leads to murder; while sadness becomes despair, and if unregulated, leads to suicide.

Some people haven't recognized the connection between anger and sadness or the destructive power each of them have. Perhaps the problems posed by sadness are more readily identified. Sometimes deep hurt or unresolved loss results in such a profound sadness that it permeates all of the victim's life. This pall of pessimism can settle into a person's psyche, impacting not only his or her attitude toward life but also chemicals in the brain in such a way as to produce persistent depression. Some psychologists call depression "anger turned inward." Such internal misery, focused on the regrets of life, makes it very difficult or impossible for us to be forgiving.

Anger turned outward causes its own set of problems. It's true that sometimes it can be helpful, as when becoming angry helps us to protect our values or our sense of fairness and kindness. Anger can stop abuse and protect the vulnerable. It can counterbalance depression, identifying painful realities that need attention.

But anger that lashes out selfishly to hurt those who didn't intend to offend creates problems rather than solves them. Anger can be a powerfully destructive force. Justified or not, anger uncontrolled soon overwhelms us.

Most of us resist applying the words *anger* and *rage* to our frustrations. Like me, you probably have moments when you get irritated with those who waste your time, who ignore or depreciate your questions, or who tease or ridicule you. You'd probably acknowledge that you occasionally get upset. But few of us like to admit to becoming *angry,* and we quickly reject the suggestion that what we are feeling is *rage.*

Quibbling over what word describes the level of our displeasure reveals our defensiveness about this subject. Most of us have learned to mask our anger. We hide it well from those we know the least and from those who have power over us—supervisors, employers, teachers, law enforcement officers, and so on. We're most likely to let it loose among those we know the best and care about the most.

The more open I am to accepting my anger, the more aware I am of it. That's humbling for me. My quick frustration at a hotel charge that the clerk said wouldn't be added to my bill but that showed up on the final statement reminds me. My impatience with the driver who sits in front of me far into the green light and then eases ahead at half the speed limit when I'm in a hurry reminds me. The telephone help-desk operator who thinks she knows the answer to my question before she listens to it reminds me.

I see it in others too—in their tight jaws, their squinting eyes, their loud and harsh words, and their rough treatment of children and animals. Anger not only identifies our values, it betrays our prejudices, our past hurts, our defenses, our vulnerabilities. And no matter what prompts it, uncontrolled anger limits our ability to reason. It freezes our mental processes and makes it nearly impossible for us to listen and learn. It destroys relationships and paralyzes community and societal progress. It is destructive rather than protective and leads to suspicion, animosity, mistrust, hatred, and revenge.

Ideally, we learn to accept both anger and sadness as helpful emotions. Whenever one is present, so is the other, even if we don't immediately recognize it. Societal and cultural norms sometimes blunt our awareness of this reality. For example, imagine a little boy playing with a hammer at his daddy's workbench. What does he do if he hits his thumb with the hammer? He cries and runs to Mommy or Daddy for comfort! But imagine what his daddy does if *he* hits *his* thumb with that hammer. He either curses in anger or ignores the pain, right? "Big boys don't cry." Society has conditioned him to avoid sadness, conditioning him instead to express his anger with profanity or to ignore his feelings entirely.

A better reaction would be to balance one extreme with the other. When someone has hurt us and our anger is threatening to go out of control, we can lessen its power by counter-balancing it with the sadness we feel because of the attack. And when sadness smothers optimism and hope, we need to reclaim some of the anger the offense has stirred up to refresh our energy and prevent depression. In that way one becomes the director of one's own life, the conductor of emotional balance and health. That balance produces many positive results, including better physical health and stronger relationships.

The fourth R is revenge. The pursuit of revenge also prevents forgiving. We want the offender to hurt as we hurt. We want him or her to feel the pain they made us feel. The desire to hurt those who have hurt us comes naturally to us human beings. At best, the threat of suffering revenge can support justice and turn people away from harming others. But in general, people seem to find it nearly impossible to keep to those lofty intentions, and our revenge ends up simply as retribution instead.

While the quick pursuit of justice is beneficial, continuing to hold on to negative feelings over a long period takes a serious toll on us. Eventually, it will consume us. To take revenge on someone who has hurt us—to really do it well— takes time, lots of time. Deciding what you're going to do, looking for the opportunity to do it, carrying out the scheme, and then watching to see whether what you've done had the desired effect—all this can absorb months or years. And all that time you have linked yourself to the one you dislike so intensely! Instead of forgetting them or ignoring them, you've become preoccupied with them, carrying them around with you everywhere you go, and even bringing them into the places you consider special, only to let them rob you of relaxation and peace.

The emotional investment we make in seeking revenge is large too. It may begin with just a flash of irritation, but anger grows when it's been harbored and nurtured. Wounds kept open fester and grow, pushing us to make even greater efforts to lash back at the offender. We want to relieve our pain and protest the disrespect, and we think revenge is the way to do that.

But our quest for relief and recognition often ends in disappointment, because the other people in our life seem to ignore us or even to side with the perpetrator. And when that happens, the pain we feel increases exponentially. It suggests that we're in the wrong.

If our attempts to make the offender's life miserable don't bring sadness or grief or suffering or apology from them, we either accept failure or double our efforts to inflict damage. Emotional ups and downs mark the journeys of those who are bent on revenge. On one hand, plotting how to get revenge and anticipating how we'll feel if we're successful creates excitement, while any pleasant or successful event in the offender's life makes us miserable. Over time, we work to maintain the fevered pitch of our disdain, picking at our wound, which makes it hurt and thus motivates us to persist. Eventually, we'll become preoccupied and perhaps even obsessed with attacking the perpetrator. And perpetuating the anger eventually breeds bitterness and contributes to our unhappiness. We're drinking the poison and expecting the perpetrator to die.

That point is powerfully made in the movie *The Interpreter*. Nicole Kidman plays the role of Silvia, a white African whose parents were killed during the racial conflict that eventually ended apartheid in the fictional country of Moboto. Silvia leaves the country, grows up, and becomes an interpreter who works at the United Nations.

Eventually, the black man responsible for the death of her parents becomes president of Moboto. While he's preparing for his first trip to deliver a speech at the United Nations, the Secret Service learns of a plot to assassinate him. Silvia, of course, is the prime suspect. While being interviewed by Sean Penn's character, a Secret Service agent, she tells this story.

> Everyone who loses somebody wants revenge on someone. On God if they can't find anyone else. And in Africa, . . . in Moboto, the Ku believe that the only way to end grief is to save a life. If someone is murdered, a year of mourning ends with a ritual that we call "the drowning man trial." There's an all-night party beside a river. At dawn, the killer is put in a boat. He's taken out on the water and he's dropped. He's bound, so he can't swim. The family of the dead then has to make a choice. They can let him drown, or they can swim out and save him. The Ku believe that if the family lets the killer drown, they'll have justice but spend the rest of their lives in mourning. But if they save him, if they admit that life isn't

always just, that very act can take away their sorrow. Vengeance is
a lazy form of grief.

Reality, regret, rage, and the desire for revenge all make forgiving very difficult or impossible. Other barriers exist, too, several of which fall into the category of false assumptions about forgiving. We'll talk about them later, as we learn more about forgiveness.

The next chapter explores a significant religious misunderstanding of forgiveness, and chapter 13 defines forgiveness in practical terms.

CHAPTER TWELVE

God's Gift

A friend of mine who is a professional accepted a job in a small town where only a handful of people of his race lived. He contacted a real estate agent, and they began to look at the homes that were listed as being for sale. After looking for a while, they found one that appealed to him, so he asked his agent to make an offer on it. But when the agent passed the offer along to the owners of the house, they turned it down, saying they had decided not to sell their house after all.

So, my friend and the agent continued their search, making offers on several other houses. But one would-be seller after another rejected the offers. Apparently, all the local citizens there who a day or two before intended to move had changed their minds and now were contented to stay where they were. Not likely, is it?

What was my friend's response? He just kept searching until eventually he found someone who was willing to sell to him. Some people in the neighborhood of the house that he bought didn't want him and his family there, but they moved in anyway and made significant professional and personal contributions to the community.

In my view, my friend's attitude and actions were a living example of something Jesus told His disciples: "You have heard that it was said, 'Eye for eye, and tooth for tooth.' But I tell you, do not resist an evil person. If anyone slaps you on the right cheek, turn to them the other cheek also. And if anyone wants to sue you and take your shirt, hand over your coat as well. If anyone forces you to go one mile, go with them two miles" (Matthew 5:38–41).

Jesus gave this directive in northern Palestine, near the Sea of Galilee and the town of Capernaum. There was a Roman garrison nearby. It was a concrete reminder of Jewish military and political weakness, implying that the God of the Jews wasn't strong enough to protect His people. And the presence of the Roman garrison there brought with it the intrusion of pagans into the Jewish community, the immorality that typically springs up near army posts that are far from home, and the cruelty with which the Romans imposed their will on an unwilling population.

For years these harsh realities generated resentments. Brooding discontent led to guerilla activity that occasionally flashed into active protest or attacks. And every time the Jews rebelled against the occupying Romans, their rebellion was met with harsh reprisals.

The Jews longed for relief from their oppressors. That's why Jesus' charisma and miraculous powers seized their attention. Might Jesus be the one to overthrow the Romans? Was He the answer to their dreams and prayers? Was He their Deliverer? Would He be the one to punish the Romans for their sins, taking revenge on those enemies of God?

On one occasion, after Jesus had spent some time with massive curious crowds, He had withdrawn, taking His closest followers with Him so He could teach them about His kingdom. Catch their excitement! Picture the "war masks" etched on their faces by the decades of disrespect they'd had to swallow, the confiscation and destruction of their property, the erosion of their moral and community values, the personal slights and taunts, and the conscriptions into temporary service by even the lowest-ranking Roman soldiers. Imagine the elation they felt when they saw Jesus' miracles and thought themselves on the verge of attaining freedom from bondage, of gaining control, of avenging themselves on their oppressors!

Then think about how they felt when Jesus said they were not to look for justice of the "eye for an eye, and tooth for a tooth" kind, or even to resist an evil person. Instead, they were to turn the other cheek and to go the second mile.

Are followers of Jesus really supposed to take these instructions literally? Did He really mean that we shouldn't resist evil or protest injustice or protect ourselves when attacked? Is it never appropriate to push back against the encroachment of sinful aggressors?

Various interpretations

People have taken several different approaches to answering these questions. Some say Jesus is expressing the ideal, the standard we should strive to reach. Our limitations as fallen human beings will prevent us from ever actually reaching this level of moral living, but we just have to do the best we can.

Others believe that Jesus was using hyperbole—exaggeration—a literary device familiar to the Jews. They say Jesus didn't mean for us to take what He said literally. He was just laying out a principle that we should apply as best we can—God doesn't expect us to actually go to the extreme He pictured.

Still others say Jesus did mean His instructions to be taken literally. He was telling them the best way to handle the situation they were in. Resisting a Roman soldier's command would trigger his anger, and increasing one's resistance in turn would ultimately lead to violence and death. The Romans had the weapons and the forces to use them. Resistance was futile. It was better to cope by resigning oneself to that fact, being compliant, and thus staying alive.

And then there are those who see these words of Jesus as prescriptive. They believe He was saying that rather than literally fighting evil—as in evil people—or passively surrendering to it, they should actively oppose evil, but in a nonviolent way. Acting in such a way as to shine a spotlight on evil would shock even the perpetrators of that evil while also appealing to the best in them.

Those who have taken this approach of nonviolent activism—among them Mahatma Gandhi and Martin Luther King Jr.—have based it on their understanding of what Jesus told His disciples. They developed sit-ins and other forms of peaceful protest that shine the spotlight that reveals evil on the offenders they are opposing, attempting to appeal to whatever good the oppressors still have within themselves.

Some people see Jesus' words to be a call for a passive approach, but Jesus resisted evil actively and sometimes forcefully. His cleansing of the temple is a dramatic example of this. It wasn't a meek, passive, compliant Jesus who cleansed the temple, but rather a very intense and determined Jesus, much more like the one His followers had been longing for when He called them to join Him. John described Jesus' demeanor in these forceful terms: "Zeal for your house consumes me" (John 2:17; cf. Psalm 69:9).

So, answering the question of what Jesus would do is not as simple as reading the injunction from the Sermon on the Mount and applying it literally. It does seem clear that Jesus intends to preserve spiritual and moral values, including our advocating for those who can't protect themselves. But the question of how best to do that gets varying responses.

In an airport terminal recently an illustration of the complexity of applying

The Several Forms of Justice

The word *justice* is used in several ways, each of which is important to the full concept. Because these forms of justice are not mutually exclusive, an individual can "experience" several of them simultaneously. I've listed below various forms of justice with a brief description of each.

- *Punitive justice* imposes some kind of arbitrary penalty on the perpetrator. The penalty isn't necessarily related to the crime; the intent is to impress on those who experience this kind of justice the seriousness of their deeds and to impose punishment on them.

- *Retributive justice* goes a step beyond punitive justice, having the intent of making the perpetrator hurt in the way he or she has hurt the victim. The "eye for an eye, tooth for a tooth" quest for revenge illustrates this facet of justice.

- *Compensatory justice* is explicitly tied to the crime; the perpetrator is required to pay back to the victim what he or she took from the victim. This form of justice works well in cases of robbery and theft but is also sometimes assessed in cases of personal injury and assault, to aid in the victim's recovery or to compensate the victim for the loss of time or opportunities or the use of limbs or other parts of the victim's body.

- *Preventative justice* looks to the future. It imposes restrictions on the perpetrators designed to preclude them from repeating those crimes. For example, the authorities may jail people who continue to drive while inebriated—not just as a punishment but also to prevent them from injuring or killing others by keeping them off the road.

- *Restorative justice* focuses on rehabilitation of the perpetrator. Expanding beyond simple compensation for their crime, this type of justice aims to develop positive social values in the perpetrator. Restorative prison programs train inmates in how to think clearly, reason morally, act responsibly, and prepare themselves to be trustworthy citizens and to live productively in society.

those principles imposed itself on me. I was standing in a long line that led to the place where our carry-on baggage would be examined, and right behind me was a family composed of a father, a mother, and two small children.

Managing the several bags this family had brought for their journey was a significant challenge. Caring for the infant fully occupied the mother, so she wasn't able to help, and the toddler was too young help, so the dad had to move the bags along while also corralling the toddler. These tasks were stressful enough in themselves, but it seemed likely that they were preceded by the tasks of getting the family up and dressed and transported to the airport. It was apparent that the dad's patience, if he had any, was running out.

When the toddler became distracted and began to wander, the dad corrected her loudly a couple times and then he blew up. In what seemed likely to be a pattern he had followed before, he grabbed the little girl and, shouting loudly enough for all of us in the line and others far down the terminal to hear, said, *"I told you to stand still. Now, stand there and don't move!"* By then the little girl was sobbing, the mom was backing toward the end of their trail of baggage, and the baby was beginning to whimper.

What would Jesus have done if He'd been there in the flesh? Would He have kept silent and let the helpless little girl suffer the tirade of a father who couldn't control his anger? Would He have surmised that this display of anger was tempered by the public setting, and that in private this man was probably even more abusive? Would He have said something, done something, to help the father see how his own loss of control modeled what he was punishing in his daughter? Would Jesus have reached out to a clearly hurt and intimidated wife and mother? Would He have offered to help with the children and bags to relieve some of the stress? Would He have "forgiven" the man for his outburst and for the demeaning abuse of his family toward which the outburst pointed, or would He have found some way to confront the man? Or would Jesus have kept His distance, not interfering in the lives of these people?

Does forgiving mean letting evil have its way?

I can't imagine that Jesus, the Creator, wouldn't have noticed and addressed incidents like this one. How could He stand by while human beings, the crown of His creation, were mistreated? How could He have condoned by His silence attacks on the personhood and Godlikeness of human beings? Would He not have spoken up for the weak here as He did for the blind man who called for help from the side of the road? Would He not have noticed and addressed the needs of the powerless in that line as He did the woman with the unrelenting menstrual flow? Would He not have reached out to the disadvantaged there as He reached out to the neglected, the disrespected, and the shunned when He was on earth? Surely, He would have done something to help those in need!

After Jesus returned to heaven, one of His brothers described true religion by telling us what those who had it would do. He wrote, "Pure and undefiled religion before God and the Father is this: to visit orphans and widows in their trouble, and to keep oneself unspotted from the world" (James 1:27, NKJV).

Some people would have us believe that to have a forgiving spirit, we mustn't intervene, we mustn't confront evil, we mustn't do anything to stop violence, we must allow the moral fabric of society to shred without actively opposing it. But this idea is contrary to the very basis of Jesus' kingdom instructions. He commissioned His followers to be His representatives. He commissioned them to spread the truth about God all over the world and to influence society to return to God's ways. That surely must include raising awareness of inhumane and disrespectful treatment of others. So, Jesus cannot have intended us to have a passive stance toward evil and destructive behavior.

Our natural impulse to stop the mistreatment of people, to protect God's creatures, His creation, is God-given. And it is just as appropriate for us to feel that impulse when we are the ones who are being mistreated as when it involves others. When Jesus said we should love others as we love ourselves, He was describing an inherent reality. God created us to be aware of assaults on those He created in His own image, so it is appropriate for us to attempt to protect both others and ourselves. Forgiving, then, cannot mean that we must refrain from doing anything to confront the onslaught of evil.

God's gift or our task?

The Bible's story of our past hardly begins before mistrust separates human beings from God, from one another, and even within themselves. That alienation brought the need for forgiveness—otherwise the separation from God would have been eternal. Early in the book of Genesis, God announces His solution, a plan laid before the foundation of the world (see 1 Peter 1:20; Revelation 13:8). The Creator, God Himself, would come as the divine Father's Son. He would live as a humble human being, and, like an innocent lamb, be sacrificed—thus reconciling the world to Himself (see Colossians 1:20). To point forward to His coming and to graphically illustrate the high cost of forgiving, God instituted the ceremonial sacrifice of real lambs.

Periodically, however, people focused so completely on the symbol that they lost sight of the One toward whom the symbol pointed. They forgot that sacrifices of lambs didn't save those who offered them. And since those who led out in these services were responsible for seeing that they were continued, they began to see themselves as the givers of God's gift. And then people looked to their own works rather than to God's work to provide their salvation. Forgiving became *their* work.

We who live after Jesus' incarnation risk falling into a similar error—not because we rely on offering animal sacrifices, of course, but because we rely on our own ability to forgive. A common Christian misconception about forgiving rises from a misunderstanding of a fundamental instruction that Jesus gave. It comes from no less a place than the Lord's Prayer, where the way a line is worded prompts many to perceive forgiving as their task, a human task. That line says we are to pray "forgive us our debts, as we forgive our debtors" (Matthew 6:12, NKJV).

Admittedly, here Jesus Himself enjoins us to forgive. It appears that the text says we are to ask God to forgive us our debts in the way that we forgive our debtors. Worded as it is, this line suggests that God waits for us to act before He acts. If we will forgive people who have injured us, then God will forgive us. A French line speaks of a similar step-by-step process. *"Au fur et à mesure,"* it says. "In concert, we move together." You make a move, and God makes a move. You take a step, and He takes a step. You move first, and He follows. You initiate, and He reacts. You move first, and He responds. You forgive your enemies, and then God forgives you. You do your work first, and then God does His.

The New International Version reflects the flavor of Matthew's verb choice more forcefully, reinforcing the impression that forgiving is a human work. It reads "forgive us our debts, as we also have forgiven our debtors." And Luke's version of the prayer is even more direct than that of Matthew. According to Luke, Jesus told us to pray, "Forgive us our sins, for we also forgive everyone who sins against us" (Luke 11:4).

But how can this be? God has already acted! God initiated the plan of salvation and gave Himself as the reality of forgiveness. How then can the text say that we go first and God follows? That we initiate and God responds? No! God doesn't follow our lead. God isn't waiting for us to act. God doesn't rely on us; we rely on Him. Surely, forgiveness doesn't depend on us!

This view of the Lord's Prayer conflicts with the Christian view of salvation. We believe that God gave forgiveness and salvation as a gift, not as payment for our good behavior. How could a gracious God hold over us the threat that if we don't behave correctly, if we don't first forgive those who owe us or have hurt us, He won't forgive us? To require us to forgive as a condition of being forgiven would be to require us to earn salvation by our works. We would be responsible for placating God; for winning Him over; for proving to Him what worthy persons we are; and for presenting our forgiving others as justification for Him to forgive us. How could that square with the long-standing Christian proclamation of salvation by grace?

In the context of Scripture

In order to understand any biblical message correctly, we must consider it in the context of the book of which it is a part and in the circumstances in which it was originally transmitted. But we can't stop there. We must also see it in the perspective of all the other messages of the Bible. When we study the Lord's Prayer that way, we find important principles that lead us to a helpful understanding of what He meant by what He said about forgiveness.

When humans first sinned, God promised that He would intervene on their behalf. From then on, humans have looked back to that promise and forward to the coming of the Deliverer, the Savior, the Messiah. The apostles—and all of us who walk the path they trod—look back to that unique intervention of God in human history as His way of delivering us, of granting us what we couldn't obtain for ourselves. The predominant view in Scripture is clearly that salvation comes by the grace of God rather than by the works of human beings. In that context, what might this apparently aberrant section in the Lord's Prayer mean?

The immediate context tells us several important things. First, the prayer, including the section on forgiveness, is part of Jesus' instructions to His disciples. He was casting a vision of who they were, how they were to act, and what would identify them as His followers. What He says about forgiveness is part of the vision of what could happen. The disciples had chosen to follow Him, which means that they had determined to be like Him. Among God's followers, love and acceptance of one another is a given. Members of His community will reflect their leader, and the community will be known for the love they have for each other.

Second, the disciples were already saved since they had chosen to follow Jesus. As His people, then, they wished to become more Godlike. Their forgiveness of others would be evidence that God's forgiveness of them had changed them—that He had replaced their resentments of others, which are natural to humans, with His grace. Thus, a forgiving attitude toward others becomes a tool that enables us to examine ourselves rather than becoming a standard that we must attain. Instead of being a threat to our salvation that we must fight off by ourselves, it is an indication that our connection with God needs to be refreshed.

Third, Jesus is describing reality, not setting up a requirement. He is pointing out that until we experience what it is like to be forgiven by God, we won't be able to enjoy the depth of freedom and peace that comes from forgiving others. When we experience God's forgiveness, we feel real peace. And when we feel that peace, it's natural for us to share it with those who have offended us.

Mark also describes Jesus as saying something that could be taken as meaning that God waits for us to forgive other people for what they've done to us before He will forgive us for our offenses against Him. Specifically, Jesus says, "When you stand praying, if you hold anything against anyone, forgive them, so that your Father in heaven may forgive you your sins" (Mark 11:25).

In Mark's telling of this story, as in the Lord's Prayer, it initially appears that Jesus is saying God will forgive us only if we will forgive others first. But remember the indisputable clarity of the gospel message—God forgives first. He doesn't wait until we have fulfilled any conditions. God gives us forgiveness before we deserve it, while we're still sinners (see Romans 5:8).

If we read these texts quickly and superficially, not connecting them with Scripture's predominant view of salvation, we will come to believe that forgiving is our work instead of God's. Once we start down that road, forgiveness becomes a human accomplishment rather than a divine gift. Then we're likely to claim as our achievement what in actuality is God's doing. That comes very close to what Scripture defines as blasphemy.

When we have fully experienced God's forgiveness, we will know the full freedom that comes with forgiving others. Being forgiven makes us forgiving. Neither an obligation nor our accomplishment, forgiveness fulfills the vision of what can be. It provides a self-diagnostic test of our connection with Christ, and a description of the reality of a life in Him.

Forgiving is God's gift to us.

CHAPTER THIRTEEN

What Forgiveness Is— and What It Isn't

Deciding what to include and what to leave out when one talks or writes or reads about forgiveness is more complicated than you might think. When a group of us submitted a paper on forgiveness to a research journal, the peer reviewers wanted us to explain why we described the impact of forgiveness only on survivors and not on perpetrators—a worthy question. Both groups are certainly important, and both are directly affected by forgiveness.

Survivors who grant forgiveness experience significant benefits. Hundreds of research studies, scores of books, several documentaries, and untold numbers of speeches, presentations, and workshops substantiate that. Those who forgive reduce their level of stress, enhance their level of well-being, measurably improve their health and longevity, unchain themselves from the offender, and free themselves to focus their creative attention on the present and future rather than on the past. Forgiving does benefit the survivor!

But perpetrators benefit from forgiveness too. Many of them are burdened with regret, and they grieve over their misdeeds. Constantly carrying the burden of guilt weighs on them, and they suffer physical, mental, relational, and spiritual consequences. Being forgiven brings them a sense of relief and enables them to live life unfettered by the burden of their past. Even if the tangible consequences of their misdeeds don't go away—even if they must still serve prison time, for example—they are much more likely to serve "good time," as they say. They have reason to have hope, to be optimistic about what they can become. They savor the refreshing power of forgiveness.

The two facets of forgiveness—forgiveness of others and forgiveness of oneself—are closely connected and in some ways parallel to one another, but my attention was drawn to the perspective of the survivor first because of our experiencing Shannon's murder. We had to learn to cope with the emptiness brought by her death, with our imaginings of what she must have been thinking and feeling as she was being killed, with seeing in court the man who confessed to killing her. I was so absorbed in sorting through my own reactions to our loss that for some time I wasn't able to distance myself enough from my own pain to think seriously about her killer.

The word *forgiveness* itself fosters the confusion. It names an abstract concept, a category, or an idea. (Watch out for the English class review session here!) In order to become personal, forgiveness must be attached to someone—and even then it remains distant, something granted or received by a person but not part of the person herself or himself.

Only when one becomes personally involved, when one has a reason for granting forgiveness or being forgiven does it cease to be theoretical. Only when one is faced with the bitterness and anger that a survivor feels or when one is ravaged by the guilt brought by being an offender does forgiveness become tangible and intensely practical. Then, jerked down from the realm of distant theory, one experiences it in a very concrete and personal way.

To label this activity *forgiveness* seems to isolate it from us, to depersonalize its importance and depreciate its value. It too easily lets us avoid the emotional impact the situation has on us and allows us to retreat to the safer realm of intellectual examination. Feelings frighten us—particularly intense feelings and especially intense negative feelings. Anger, resentment, bitterness, grief, guilt, depression, and rage or sadness sometimes seem overwhelming. They disrupt our daily lives and relationships. They discourage and demoralize us.

In contrast, thinking seems much friendlier. It's predictable, mature, and controlled. Reason, after all, is what distinguishes us from animals, and human beings are best served when they govern their lives, choices, and relationships by reason rather than by emotion. But reason without emotion makes a person mechanistic, robotic, and diminished as a human being. Think of the challenges that the character named Data faced on the *Star Trek* TV series. The combination of Data's unlimited mental capacity and his lack of feelings produced uncertainties and confusion that he couldn't resolve on his own. He needed the help of the other crewmembers—real people. And then note the contrast between the purely intellectual Data and R2-D2—a robot character in the *Star Wars* movies, but one that was more humanlike because it had feelings. Reason benefits us when it is influenced by emotion. Whether our feelings are those of a survivor or of a perpetrator, facing them makes the distant, theoretical idea of forgiveness very tangible and important. Then *forgiveness,* the concept, becomes *forgiving,* the act by a human being.

Verbs, gerunds, and adjectives fit this perspective better than do nouns. *Forgiving* and *forgiven* makes us think of a gracious act, the caring and thoughtful person who does what is named, or the fortunate one who receives its benefits. *Forgiveness* is what is granted or received. One describes the person, "who," while the other describes the "what." One defines people; the other defines a thing, an idea.

In order to work well, particularly in difficult situations, forgiveness must become very personal, a part of our identity. Those who forgive are profoundly affected by their action—their lives are changed. Anger, resentment, and emotional pain begin to shrivel. The result is that those who forgive become forgiving people, and the attitude of those who are forgiven changes their view of themselves. Instead of being overwhelmed by regrets and guilt or by a sense of helplessness and hopelessness, they feel loved, respected, accepted, and valued.

Forgiving is the inner attitude that releases guilty perpetrators from their deeds. To survivors, forgiving means they no longer seek to punish the perpetrators for their offenses. To perpetrators, forgiving means that they accept the forgiveness offered to them. (Some prefer to call this "forgiving themselves"—a notion I resist for reasons I'll explain in a later chapter.) For both survivors and perpetrators, this may sound hopelessly idealistic—a stretch toward a fantasy world that ignores the reality of deep injury and the resulting pain. The conclusion that people never actually reach this level of forgiving is built on a misunderstanding of what forgiving actually is. In the remainder of this chapter, we'll explore what forgiving is not and what it is.

Forgiving isn't . . .

Forgiving isn't forgetting. An old Christian song began with the words "Wonderful, wonderful Jesus; He will forgive and forget." It does seem that if we want to let go of an offense and to stop punishing the offender, we must "forgive and forget"—we must forget the deed itself. Isn't that what God has promised us through Micah? Micah wrote,

> Who is a God like you,
>> who pardons sin and forgives the transgression
>> of the remnant of his inheritance?
> You do not stay angry forever
>> but delight to show mercy.
> You will again have compassion on us;
>> you will tread our sins underfoot
>> and hurl all our iniquities into the depths of the sea (Micah 7:18, 19).

Surely that speaks of God separating us from our sins.

But reason tells us that we shouldn't offer perpetrators such radical forgiveness. Doing so would enable evil persons to perpetuate their cruel deeds. Since we're living in a sinful world, a dangerous world, we must remember offenses so that we can escape suffering from them again. It seems obvious that societies that forget all the atrocities of evil people wouldn't last long. Campaigns to prevent future atrocities call us to remember the genocides, the massacres, the assaults, and the robberies of the past. Providing preventative justice is a crucial responsibility of society. Forgetting past crimes would endanger many people.

Forgetting the evil they've done wouldn't do the perpetrators a favor either. If the responsibility for their choices were to be absolved and the consequences of their deeds removed, they would learn nothing.

Forgiving isn't forgetting.

Forgiving isn't condoning. Forgiving doesn't require either the society or the survivor to change their view of morality. Wrong is wrong, and forgiveness doesn't make what was wrong become right. To require the offended or society to classify what was an evil deed now as a good one insults the ethics of just societies and the internal sense of right with which most humans resonate.

When a governor or the president pardons someone, it may appear that the crime is merely being brushed aside as if it were still offensive and illegal but now unimportant. But pardons don't transform what were considered to be evil deeds into innocent activities. They merely mean that the punishment ceases. Pardons don't erase the offenses or purge the records. The consequences of their deeds remain. Victims of robbery haven't necessarily received what was taken from them, victims of assault still suffer from their wounds, and the murdered are still dead.*

If sin were a minor matter, something that could easily be overlooked, it wouldn't have cost God so much. But forgiveness is not a glossing over of something inconsequential. It is because sin is so consequential that only the death of Jesus, the Creator of the universe, was payment enough to be able to purchase our salvation. Jesus didn't avoid the consequences of sin nor change the standards to accommodate human evil, and one has only to look at the Cross to understand how seriously God takes it.

Forgiving isn't condoning.

Forgiving isn't excusing either. Excusing may take either of two forms. First, it may refer to someone's trying to excuse an offense by explaining why it happened—why an otherwise good person has done a bad thing. Perhaps their upbringing was faulty, or they were ignorant of the moral standard, or they misunderstood the situation. Our courts recognize that some circumstances must be taken into account in determining what sentence will be given the perpetrator. Often, charges and sentences are adjusted in cases of mental illness or accident, for example. But the deed itself need not be minimized; justice can still be served.

Some perpetrators try to excuse what they've done by blaming the victim. They defend themselves by claiming that the victims asked for what they got. We learn to do this in childhood: "Timmy took my blocks, so I took his puzzle." "She hit me, so I hit her back." "He broke my trike, so I smashed his bike." Adults say similar things: "The prostitute solicited me, so it wasn't my fault." "She wore a provocative outfit, so she's responsible for enticing me to rape her." "This child disobeyed and had to be taught a lesson." "That man wasn't respectful of me, so I had to beat him up."

This "blame the victim" form of defense is as old as this earth. It's the approach Adam and Eve used after their first sin in the Garden of Eden. Here's how the Bible tells it:

> The man said, "The woman you put here with me—she gave me some fruit from the tree, and I ate it."

---

* A related declaration, sometimes confused with pardon, occurs when new evidence proves that the convicted person was actually innocent. For example, DNA evidence has recently verified that some people who were convicted of various crimes were actually innocent. In such cases, the people are not *pardoned;* they are *exonerated.* The crime is expunged from their records, and they are legally as clear as if they had never been charged, tried, or convicted.

Then the LORD God said to the woman, "What is this you have done?"

The woman said, "The serpent deceived me, and I ate" (Genesis 3:12, 13).

Even though God promised Adam and Eve forgiveness, He didn't excuse what they had done. The consequences were imposed immediately, and they continue millennia later. God promised them forgiveness, but He allowed them and all the earthly creation to experience the natural consequences of their choices.

Forgiving isn't excusing.

Forgiveness isn't reconciling. I've worked with men and women who were abused while growing up. I've found that they often bring up the subject of reconciliation with the abuser. Many who were beaten or raped as children want no relationship with their abuser as adults. They shudder to think of themselves again in the presence of that person, and in severe cases, even the memories bring back helpless infantile responses. They often ask, "Does God expect me to reconnect with the person who abused me?" "Does forgiving mean I have to become friends with the person who tortured me?" "With the person who raped me?" "Does forgiving require reconciling?"

While reconciliation may be a worthy goal, it isn't always attainable, and it certainly isn't required. Sometimes that is true because the offender can't be trusted. Even if he or she is well intentioned, some seem unable stop offending. I'm acquainted with the story of one such man. While he was in prison, he was a model of refinement, maturity, and self-control. He began to write to a woman and then to meet with her in the visitation room. They invited a pastor to meet with them and lead them through premarital counseling. All went well through the man's incarceration and for some time after he was released on parole. He got a job and became an active member of a congregation.

Then the couple decided to begin a family. Not long after they made this decision, this man was apprehended for breaking his probation. In spite of an apparently happy marriage, he had started peeping in windows. Over the next several years he cycled through a series of imprisonments, treatments, paroles, and reoffending. He approached several women, had affairs, and seemed unable to follow his probation restrictions. His continual misdeeds made reconciliation with his family and the women and others not only impossible but also unwise. He was unreliable.

I think also of a woman I met at the California state prison where I trained. At the chapel service on a Sunday morning she ecstatically told us she was going home that week. She had been out of prison several times before only to be incarcerated again, but she was sure that she was ready to make it this time. She was determined to change the course of her life, to live above the associations and enticements that had snared her into living a life of crime. How sad she and those who trusted her must have been that in a very few weeks she was back, apparently unable to make the changes she had so fervently promised and apparently wanted to make.

Decades ago, a schoolteacher took sexual advantage of a young student. When the school's administrators discovered it, the teacher was very ashamed and repentant. He said it was the first time and promised it would never happen again. Today, the situation would be handled quite differently, but at that time the school administrators decided to give him another chance. He was an outstanding teacher, so they—thinking they were doing him and another school a favor—recommended him to another city without mentioning his sexual crime.

Only when he neared retirement did the story of his life become known. His career consisted of a series of episodes like that first one. Each victim and each school thought they were the only ones. Neither law enforcement nor the next school was ever notified. The man's promises and his good intentions convinced administrators to trust him. They "forgave" him and recommended him to someone else at a school far away, thus letting him get by without confronting his behavior—and thus allowing him to continue abusing children.

Some offenders are untrustworthy, and reconciliation with them is unwise.

The state of the individual survivor may also make reconciliation impossible. Some may not be able to cope with being in the presence of or even remotely in contact with the one who caused their pain. They need to be able to state their limitations without being pushed into premature or insincere reconciliation. Their admission should come without chagrin or a sense of failure. It simply reflects the reality of our human condition—both the truth about offenses and the truth about us.

I've heard Christians say that since we're going to live eternally with everyone who accepts salvation, we'd better get used to being with them now. They presume that forgiveness must include reconciliation or it isn't really forgiveness.

While I agree that in eternity all those whom God saves will live together happily, that time has not come yet—and won't come till all human beings are radically transformed. Perpetrators will be purged of their evil tendencies, and the wounds that their victims carry will be healed.

Here's how the apostle Paul described that change: "I declare to you, brothers and sisters, that flesh and blood cannot inherit the kingdom of God, nor does the perishable inherit the imperishable. Listen, I tell you a mystery: We will not all sleep, but we will all be changed—in a flash, in the twinkling of an eye, at the last trumpet. For the trumpet will sound, the dead will be raised imperishable, and we will be changed. For the perishable must clothe itself with the imperishable, and the mortal with immortality" (1 Corinthians 15:50–53).

None of us has yet reached that immortal state. The evil one has hurt every human being in one way or another, and trust seldom survives the horrible events and memories that may be the result. Barring a miracle, we should not expect that restoring relationships as if nothing had happened is the norm. And the separation that often results is not always bad.

Acts 15 tells about a time when two great figures of the New Testament had to part their ways. The leaders of the church in Antioch had commissioned Paul and Barnabas to take the story of Jesus to places where it was as yet unknown. Paul and Barnabas had taken John Mark with them on this trip, but the young man had deserted them and had gone home before the trip was over.

The trip had been a success, and Paul proposed that they visit the churches they had planted to strengthen them. Barnabas said he wanted to take John Mark along again, but Paul wouldn't hear of it. I can only imagine what he might have said about the homesick wimp who went home to Mommy part way through the first trip. Barnabas insisted, and Paul resisted, and the discussion became heated. In fact, the disagreement became so sharp that the two parted company. With what result? The number of evangelistic teams doubled! Paul and Barnabas each recruited helpers and went on separate trips.

But the point for our discussion here is that even Christian leaders—even the apostles of Jesus—sometimes avoid each other's company.

Forgiving isn't reconciling.

Forgiving is . . .

Forgiving is facing reality. We tend to avoid facing reality, especially when facing it is painful. It's no fun to acknowledge haunting memories—times when a spouse betrayed our trust, a business associate lied about us, a colleague misrepresented us, or a family member rejected us. We're shamed by the beatings and abuse we suffer. Reality can be cruel.

A distraught woman who came to see me said she had been diagnosed as having an incurable venereal disease. Though she hadn't been a religious person while she was growing up, she had chosen to remain a virgin till she was married—both because she wanted to keep it special and because she wanted to avoid exposing herself and her future husband to sexually transmitted diseases.

By the time this woman became an adult, she had become a Christian. She met a great Christian man, and they fell in love and were married. Then, several months after their marriage, she began having vaginal discomfort, so she made an appointment with her doctor. He told her she had a venereal disease. When this woman told her husband about the diagnosis, he admitted contracting the disease during his teens. His admission devastated her. He had been a lifelong Christian, and she presumed he had shared her firm commitment to sexual restraint. She had thought she was safe with him. Not only had his choices affected him, now they were hurting her too. And just as devastating as the disease was the fact that he hadn't told her he had the disease. By keeping that a secret, he destroyed her trust in him!

Painful memories trigger aversion. When a man I knew was in grade school, his classmates ridiculed him. Overweight and uncoordinated, he was the laughingstock of the playground. So, whenever he could, he stayed inside reading or working on the classroom computer. But he couldn't avoid the other boys forever. They still found ways to humiliate him.

As an adult he was successful in his career, but those memories still haunted him. He still didn't want to face reality. He wanted to bury those old memories where they'd never be resurrected.

Embarrassment drives many memories underground. It isn't just the perpetrators who want to hide the horrible truth. The survivors want to hide it too. Only the indiscreet or courageous volunteer the indelicacies of their painful past or unsavory present. Few muster the courage to say, "I'm an alcoholic," or "I'm an addict," or "I'm a convicted sex offender." Most who do so already feel forgiven. Their shame has been covered by the wonderful freedom of facing reality and being loved in spite of it.

Until we're able to look squarely in the face of our memories, we can't overcome them. When they're not controlled, they manage us, intimidate us, and restrict us to the parts of life that don't raise them. Or worse, they send us down the road of deceit, and we resort to covering up what we really are and hoping desperately not to be found out. That kind of life is a prison. Because we're chained to what is hurting us, we're tempted to become increasingly self-absorbed, hiding behind frenetic action or isolation. Either way, we're really miserable. The bold ones of us act out, making a spectacle of ourselves, and hoping to keep others off guard or at bay or so impressed they'd never guess the state we're in. We're desperate to keep up appearances.

The timid ones of us wear shame like a jacket. We're convinced everyone sees and ridicules our embarrassment, loathes being around us, and hates us as much as we hate ourselves. We avoid people, withdraw into our personal misery, and slump into any available corner. We're desperate to hide.

Neither approach works. The only way to health is to face realty. Painful as it seems, the kindest path to restoration lies through that dark valley. We must admit to ourselves what happened before we can choose to live above and beyond it. We can't hope until we suffer.

Psalm 23:4 addresses our reluctance to walk this tough road. David acknowledges that sometimes life is hard. He alludes to our aversion to pain, loss, and misery. And most important, he tells us how we can cope in spite of the rigors of the journey:

> Even though I walk
> through the darkest valley,
> I will fear no evil,
> for you are with me;
> your rod and your staff,
> they comfort me.

Facing the truth is not easy. Shadows haunt us when we've had a taste of the horrors that lurk there. Tragedy leaves us suspicious and anxious. But we can't avoid the truth forever. Eventually, we must walk through the valley of the shadow. Until we face the demons of our past, we cannot be truly free from them.

Many people can't face their demons alone. Before venturing into the darkness, they must find some helpful traveling companions. They need to enlist the support of trusted friends and/or trained professionals, and, as David said, the Divine Shepherd. Our trust in God is an invaluable resource that will help us through this frightening experience.

Forgiving begins with facing reality.

Forgiving means confronting the perpetrator. After we've faced the reality that is ours, we must confront the truth. Perpetrators need to be stopped, both for their own sake and for the sake of those they hurt. Confrontation mobilizes the strength of the victim, and it holds up a mirror in which the abuser can see themselves and what they've done.

Those wounded by perpetrators are often shamed into silence by the claim that they have done something wrong. Children whose parents beat them, for example, are being told over and over again that they are worthless, disobedient, and incorrigible. The abusers communicate the message that if it weren't for the abused, everything would be fine; but the abused repeatedly mess things up, ruining other's people's lives. They're told they deserve what they're getting and maybe more—they certainly don't deserve anything better. The devastation of their self-concept often impairs their accomplishments for the rest of their lives. They're left feeling valueless and inferior.

People who abuse their spouses make similar speeches, blaming their victims for causing the problem. They're blamed for forgetting to do a chore or not making the right meal or not earning enough money or making too much noise or allowing the children to think or say or do something upsetting. Whatever the excuse, the perpetrator berates and belittles the victim, making it out to be their fault and heaping humiliation on them.

Some perpetrators cycle through rage and remorse. They lose themselves in anger, but when it subsides, they become very remorseful. Feeling guilty, they apologize and ask for understanding and forgiveness, and they beg for another chance. They want to be judged on how they behave when they're compliant—not when they lose control. Add alcohol or illicit drugs to this mix, and everyone involved becomes entangled in a web of confusing emotions and long-term damage. Victims are left confused and conflicted, wanting to believe that things will change but unable to trust the good intentions of the apparently repentant abuser. Victims want to be generous, so they say we all have our faults. But their emotional and physical wounds cry out for relief and healing.

Perpetrators need to be stopped from creating this avalanche of pain. Until they are held responsible for their actions, they're unlikely to modify their behavior. Unless they are helped to see what they are doing to others and given tools to change, they have little motivation to stop their abuse. For the sake of the victims, perpetrators need to be confronted.

They need to be confronted for their own sake as well. To repeatedly blame others for one's anger or discomfort or rigidity is to avoid what is in oneself. Until the perpetrators face themselves, their own growth is slowed, and their ability to adapt and adjust to others is diminished. Their friendships suffer, as do their intimate and family relationships. Abusers either alienate other people or withdraw from close connections with them, including those outside their family circle. They become less and less open about themselves and spend more and more emotional energy covering up—hiding from themselves and from others, including God.

By confronting the offender with the reality of who they are, they offer him or her an opportunity to reclaim his or her true identity. Until such people face themselves, they cannot accept forgiveness, because in order to experience forgiveness, they must admit that they need it—they must admit that they have offended and hurt other people. They must repent of what they did and ask to be forgiven.

Matthew records what Jesus said about forgiveness in this statement from the Sermon on the Mount: "If you are offering your gift at the altar and there remember that your brother or sister has something against you, leave your gift there in front of the altar. First go and be reconciled to them; then come and offer your gift" (Matthew 5:23, 24).

Here it's clear that Jesus was speaking to offenders who have said or done something that has hurt someone. The persons who are hurt, then, have legitimate complaints against the offender; they have said or done something for which they need to repent and apologize. To come to God asking for His forgiveness before expressing sorrow and regret to the one who has been mistreated is arrogant and presumptuous. It demonstrates an insensitive disregard for the pain of others and a selfish focus on their own discomfort.

God helps offenders recognize their guilt. (More on this in the chapters that follow.) Perpetrators can't enjoy the rejuvenating freedom of being forgiven until they accept responsibility for what they've done. This isn't to say that whether perpetrators and/or their victims experience the freedom of dependence is entirely a matter of the other's response. Each can experience the freedom of forgiveness even if the other will not or cannot face the truth. Perpetrators can choose to see themselves as forgiven by God even though their victims retain their anger and resentment toward them. And victims can release the rage and resentment that chains them to the offense and to the one who has abused them even if the perpetrator won't accept responsibility and apologize for his or her actions.

As I noted earlier, some victims cannot be reconciled to the person who has offended them. Fortunately, reconciliation isn't required for the offender to experience forgiveness. In fact, both the victim and the perpetrator can have this confrontation with the truth without having any direct contact with each other. With the perpetrator or alone, victims can recognize the painful truth that they have been abused. That is their truth. And perpetrators can confess the truth that they have been unkind or cruel and they can apologize through a mediator or through a letter. They don't have to talk directly to their victims. When they confess what they have done and do what they can to make amends, they will receive God's grace—and may even experience the emotional rush that sometimes accompanies the transition from offender to forgiven sinner.

Forgiving includes confronting the truth.

Forgiveness means expecting consequences. Let's be clear about this. Forgiving doesn't solve all life's problems or remove the consequences that sinful behavior sometimes brings. The results of these tragedies continue to exist even if the perpetrators have been forgiven.

Once, on an airliner, I sat beside a man who I learned was returning from a rare trip away from home. Twenty-two years earlier, his wife had been struck by a drunk driver. That terrible accident had paralyzed her, and ever since then he had been her caregiver. Twenty-four hours a day, seven days a week, for the most part without vacations and weekends off, he attended to her needs. This constricted life, so different from whatever they had anticipated with pleasure, was the terrible consequence of someone else's irresponsibility, their sin. And it would never change in this life. They had no hope for improvement of their situation.

I wouldn't have been surprised to hear that my seatmate was miserable—and angry and resentful—because of the changes the accident had made in his life and that of his wife. But he said that he didn't carry a load of anger anymore. He wasn't going to have his life sapped away by something he couldn't control.

But victims aren't the only ones whose lives are changed by what perpetrators do. The life of the perpetrator is changed too. If their abuse is criminal, they may be imprisoned. And if they're at all sensitive, the consequences that their victims suffer combined with the damage done to their own lives make the load of shame and guilt that they carry painfully heavy. Some slide into depressions so deep that they withdraw, hunker down in shame and guilt, and not uncommonly commit suicide.

A woman who was serving time in a state prison shared her tragic story with me. She had been physically abused as a child, and to escape the pain she was experiencing at home, she got married while she was still in her teens. All was well until she had a baby. The baby was fussy, crying a lot and sleeping for only short periods at a time. The constant crying and the interruptions of their sleep wore out her husband and her. Eventually, her husband began losing control of himself. At first he just became agitated, yelling and stomping out of the house when the baby's crying upset him. Eventually, however, he became violent and began shaking and slapping the baby.

Remembering the misery she suffered as an abused child and horrified that now it was happening to her baby, this woman decided that both of them would be better off dead. So one day she took the baby and checked into a hotel. There, in the isolation of the hotel room, she played out her deadly plot. When the baby went to sleep, the woman held a pillow over its face until its life was gone. Then she took her overdose of pills and lay down to die too. But to her horror, she woke up. What she thought would be a merciful solution to her problems had instead become a horrific crime. Arrested, convicted, and sentenced, all that lay ahead of her was years and years of imprisonment. On suicide watch, constantly feeling the agony of having killed the one to whom she had given life—the one she loved more than any other—her life had become an unending nightmare.

So, why forgive if forgiving doesn't eliminate the consequences? Why face reality if doing so doesn't change it?

Why? *Because in truth there is freedom.* Jesus told us that when He said, "The truth will set you free" (John 8:32). When we hide from the truth, we bind ourselves, restricting our freedom to be who we really are. To victims, forgiveness is an invitation to face the reality of their painful past, and to offenders, it's an invitation to face the truth about themselves—though admitting that truth means accepting its consequences.

Forgiving includes expecting consequences.

Forgiving means releasing anger and resentment. This is the final step in the process.

The corrosive power of retained bitterness eats away at one's happiness, health, and vitality. Retaining anger toward someone chains us to the very person from whom we wish to be free. And retaining anger at ourselves pushes us toward depression. Both victim and perpetrator benefit when they release this pent-up hostility.

Years ago I met a young woman who had immigrated from Germany. In a group of people who were seeking spiritual and emotional healing, she disclosed her long-held frustration toward her father. Although he had been dead for many years, she was still in emotional turmoil about him.

This woman loved her dad as a father. Memories of his gentle kindness and his thoughtful care for her and the rest of his family comforted her. But during World War II, he had been an active Nazi and had served in Hitler's army. She was a child during the war, too young to understand the implications of her father's involvement with the Nazis, and he died before the full implications of what he fought for dawned on her. But when she realized that this man had advocated racial and religious bigotry, had defended ethnic superiority, and had supported the slaughter of innocent people, she was appalled! She felt betrayed by one she cherished, and now, with him gone, her feelings of shame and anger were frozen. Only when she was able to imagine a visit with him in which she spoke of her grief and other negative emotions and thought of what he might have said in response was she able to resolve her confusion and settle her tumultuous feelings.

For her very survival, the woman who smothered her baby also had to let go of anger toward herself. She had to track the process all the way through to this crucial end. Omitting this component would have left her in perpetual despair. Somehow, each of us—victim and perpetrator—has to find a way to let go of the anger and resentment connected with the offense and with the offender.

Harboring resentment does nothing to change the reality of what has happened. Nor does denying the truth, avoiding the deed and/or the doer, or pretending there are no consequences. Somehow the emotions stirred by the event must be resolved. In order for forgiving to be effective, we must find a way to release anger and resentment.

Forgiving is not forgetting, condoning, excusing, or reconciling. Instead, it means facing the truth, confronting the perpetrator, expecting consequences, and releasing anger and resentment.

But, as all those who have struggled to forgive know, it is much easier to list these things than to do them. How we can do them is the subject of the next chapter.

CHAPTER FOURTEEN

Human Tasks

Willing is not doing. To wish for something to happen does not make it happen. This is as true of forgiveness as of any other part of life. The old proverb says it well: "The road to hell is paved with good intentions." *Wanting* good things to happen doesn't make them happen.

That's so true of forgiveness! Many wish to let go of their burdensome anger and resentment, their guilt and remorse, but it seems that they just can't do it. Why can't they? Why can't they find forgiveness?

Misunderstanding is one reason. People misunderstand what forgiveness is and seek their faulty version. When what they find isn't what they expected—for example, when the victim and the perpetrator aren't reconciled or when a criminal perpetrator is sentenced to prison, some people assume the two parties haven't found forgiveness. We have seen that's not always the case. Forgiveness doesn't necessarily remove the consequences that the offense brings.

Some also neglect or refuse to do what brings about the freedom of forgiveness. In many cases, even when those involved understand that truth and consequences shape the experience of forgiveness, they cannot forgive their perpetrators or accept forgiveness themselves if they've been the parties at fault. This chapter and the two that follow point toward the solution of that problem. This chapter will describe some tangible things we can do to be forgiving and forgiven. The next chapter describes Jesus as the model Forgiver, and the following chapter explains what God can do when our best efforts to follow Jesus' example fail.

Adjust your perception

When we are devastated by loss or injury, our immediate inclination is to assume that we are in a unique situation—and consequently, that we're worthy of special consideration and help. Healthy people raised in healthy families learn that early on. Good parents protect vulnerable children, stand up for them when they are abused, soothe them when they are hurt, and bandage their wounds when they are injured. So, when as adults we are hurt or offended, it is natural for us to expect to be treated in that way.

Now, openness to receiving the help and support that others are willing to give isn't a bad thing. Gestures of friendship remind us that we don't have to face painful circumstances alone. Other people do empathize with us, and their comfort can encourage us as we reorient our lives for the future.

But it isn't helpful for us to become so complacent that we depend on others for our survival. People who are dependent wait for others to act. Their recovery hinges on what other people can or cannot do for them. Eventually, those who follow this practice become passive and submit themselves to others rather than determining their own fate. They become stuck.

The opposite extreme is equally paralyzing. Those who refuse to accept the reality of their situation pretend either that the injury did not happen or that it had no effect on them. In either case, they can't move forward because they can't deal with something that they won't face. Unrealistic confidence that they can live as if nothing happened produces a large blind spot and blunts their relational, emotional, physical, or spiritual lives—or some combination of them. They cannot be whole until they adjust their perception.

Soon after our daughter Shannon was killed, a gracious call from a rabbi friend triggered such an adjustment for me. He expressed his sadness at our loss of a daughter. That touched me. Later, upon reflecting on his call, I was humbled by his thoughtful empathy with us over the loss of one child when he could make a lengthy list of the relatives of his who were massacred in the Holocaust! Who was I to think my situation was the worst possible reality anyone has ever faced? In a strange but very helpful way, his call left Barbara and me feeling grateful that our loss wasn't greater than it was. It kept us from feeling forever sorry for ourselves—paralyzed by our misfortune and dependent on others to pick up the pieces of our lives.

Those thoughts surfaced again when Barbara and I went to Dover Air Force Base to accompany the families who had gathered there to meet the airplane that was bringing home the bodies of their children who died in the attack on the USS *Cole*. Those thoughts recurred again when I visited with survivors of the 9/11 terrorist attacks and held services for some who were killed on that day. Certainly, sharing the loss that others experienced renewed memories of our own loss. But at the same time it reminded us that we are not alone. Others know our grief and share our sorrow. And because we know that others have endured life's challenges and survived—and even thrived—we, too, can embrace our sorrow, and by our hope in God and with the wisdom He gives, we can make something good out of all the bad stuff that has happened. Paul's words in Romans 8:28 echo that sentiment: "We know that in all things God works for the good of those who love him, who have been called according to his purpose."

This approach illustrates what Fred Luskin and other helpful instructors say in more forceful terms. They encourage us to stop whining and instead to go out to reclaim the territory that the offender has attempted to take. They encourage us to assert ourselves, to confront the situation, and describe our response to it in "I" messages ("I am upset that you blame me for this") rather than "you" messages ("You upset me when you tell me it's my fault"). They urge us to invite those who are hurting us to change, and they remind us to follow through on consequences if the perpetrators won't change. They also tell us that we need to learn what we can change and what we can't change.

All of this is very good advice. These counselors point out ways we can recover control over our own lives and choose how we will live from now on. And they require us to shift our picture of ourselves from victim to survivor.

Restore love

Most of us have heard the lofty advice that we should "hate the sin but love the sinner." That is much easier said than done. How can I bring myself to love someone who has been mean and disrespectful to me? How can I love someone who has abused or humiliated me? Why would anyone suggest that I love the perpetrator who has hurt me?

To understand, we must define what we mean by *love*. We are not, of course, talking of romantic affection that attracts us to the one we "love." Instead, we're considering the principled recognition of someone other than ourselves as a person of worth. Their worth isn't based on how kind or thoughtful they are. The respect and affection we give them doesn't come because of how wise or disciplined or helpful they are. They are valued because they are God's creation. And they are individuals for whom Christ died. God doesn't love them—or us—because we deserve His love. He loves us in spite of ourselves, because we are His creation, His children.

This recognition is embedded in an early Bible story of confrontation and anger, resentment and revenge. Two brothers, Cain and Abel, lived contrasting lives. The book of Genesis describes Abel as a gentle man, compliant with God's suggestions, while Cain was innovative and creative—and he chafed at the instructions God gave.

Scripture says God told them to bring an offering, so the brothers each brought one. Abel brought what God asked for them to bring, while Cain brought something he had put a lot of effort into, something in which he was deeply invested, but it wasn't what God told them to bring. How surprised Cain was when God accepted Abel's offering and rejected his! He resented what he considered to be a slight and became so jealous of Abel that he plotted his murder and then carried out what he had plotted.

God confronted Cain and asked where his brother was. "I don't know," Cain replied. "Am I my brother's keeper?" (see Genesis 4:9). His question implied that God should answer, "No, you are not your brother's keeper." That would make sense, wouldn't it? Brothers don't have keepers. Zoos have keepers. Bees have keepers. Stables have keepers. Pets and gardens, soccer goals and prisons have keepers. Keepers supervise those under their control. Keepers take care of those who can't care for themselves. Keepers are in charge of that which they keep.

But in making his insolent reply, Cain missed a crucial truth. It was true that he wasn't his brother's keeper. But he was his brother's *brother*. Brothers are equals, born of the same parents, loved by the same family. Brothers encourage one another, share with one another, support one another, and protect one another. In killing Abel, Cain hadn't been an unfaithful keeper; he had failed to be a loving brother.*

---

* Seminary teacher Gerhard Hasel was the first person I heard point out this crucial lesson.

Scripture repeatedly says that all who accept God and follow Him are His children. For that reason, believers often refer to one another as "brothers" and "sisters." In many ways, our affinity and loyalty to one another equals what we do and how we feel about those who are literally of the same blood.

Because God is the source of all that is, through Him we are all connected to one another. From that perspective, it is a little stretch for us to see ourselves as linked to all the members of the human race. Each and every human being is—all of us are—brothers and sisters to one another. As such, recognition of the intrinsic worth of every human being is a given.

This distinction between behavior and worth is crucial. Without it we cannot let go of the anger, resentment, and desire for revenge that we feel toward those who have disrespected and abused others or us. Our connection to one another—and even our recognizing the value of each person—starts us in the right direction. It does not, however, do away with the need to be truthful and to expect aberrant behavior to have consequences.

Then for us to smile at someone who was beating a child, to love someone who continued to steal or destroy others' property, to affirm someone who betrayed, defamed, and maliciously murdered reputations or people is clearly out of bounds. These deeds must be confronted and condemned. To prevent further damage, either the abuse must stop or the perpetrator must be restricted. Doing so sets us up as "keepers" of offenders, superior to them and no longer equally valuable members of the human family. On the basis of destructive behavior, just such a distinction may need to be drawn, but if that distinction creeps into our assumptions about the intrinsic worth of every individual, we re-create a repressive elevation of those presumed to be superior over those judged to be inferior.

Love means forgiving one's self. The kind of distinction made above is as devastating to our view of ourselves as it is for our relationships with others. Not only does this blending of intrinsic worth and behavioral performance make it impossible for us to "love the sinner but hate the sin," it makes it nearly impossible for us to value ourselves. (We'll explore this more in chapter 16, "Forgiving Ourselves.")

Distinguishing between performance and personhood is as important to our view of ourselves as it is to our view of offenders. For both, letting go of resentment, regret, rage, and the desire for revenge depends on the restoration of our belief that we have intrinsic value, which is what I call an attitude of love.

Restoring that is very difficult for most of us, but we can learn to do it. Parents can help their children by refusing to consider them to be bad boys and girls and treating them as such. Instead, they can treat them as people who have done bad things.

How can we extend that approach and restore an attitude of love toward perpetrators?

Frank Kimper described this process in a very practical way. His series of informal essays, written decades ago and never published, help the reader understand and accomplish the separation of sin from the sinner. His essays comprise part 3 of this book. I encourage you to read and reflect on them and to put them to work for you. I trust they will be as helpful to you as they have been to me—presenting a tangible way to "restore an attitude of love" toward those who have hurt us.

Be thankful

Thankfulness and gratitude destroy bitterness and resentment. They lead us to remember the good things we have. In the face of adversity, that awareness can shift our perception from horror to hope. Remember this statement made by the apostle Paul: "Rejoice in the Lord always. I will say it again: Rejoice! Let your gentleness be evident to all. The Lord is near. Do not be anxious about anything, but in every situation, by prayer and petition, with thanksgiving, present your requests to God. And the peace of God, which transcends all understanding, will guard your hearts and your minds in Christ Jesus" (Philippians 4:4–7).

Worry retreats when confronted with prayer. What a relief! Preoccupation with our pain will diminish if we approach God and make our requests to Him. Peace beyond our wildest expectations will protect our hearts and minds. What a promise!

But this prayer—don't miss this—is offered "with thanksgiving." How can we do that? By remembering the good things we have, or have experienced, and thanking God for them. This turns our mind away from despair and reminds us of better things.

As the Deputy Chief of Navy Chaplains for Reserve Matters, I visited New York City soon after 9/11. Faced with a massive pile of debris and grieving the

loss of thousands, New Yorkers were still reeling from the attack. First respond-
ers, rescue workers, and cleanup crews were respectful but resolute.

My colleague Chaplain Barry Crain went aboard a Coast Guard cutter in the
harbor guarding Manhattan and recorded Chaplain Brian Haley saying to the
ship's crew, "Dark deeds were done here a week ago, but there is sunshine today.
It's hard to see that in the darkness of midnight, but we still have to sing a song
of praise like Paul and Silas did [while in prison]. We've been encouraged as we've
heard that great anthem of our country, 'America, America, God shed His grace
on thee.' So sing your song of praise wherever it might be."

While the sadness in Yankee Stadium was palpable when the memorial prayer
service was held, the determination of New Yorkers reverberated through the
stadium as they cheered every speaker who reminded them that they would not
be defeated, that this catastrophe would not define them, that they would re-
group and rebuild. Hope in the face of disaster galvanized their determination
to prevail!

We can choose to be thankful regardless of our station in life or the tragedy of
our circumstances. While gratitude doesn't change the realities we face, it adjusts
our perception of them. In the same letter to the Philippians from which we
quoted earlier, Paul says, "I know what it is to be in need, and I know what it is to
have plenty. I have learned the secret of being content in any and every situation,
whether well fed or hungry, whether living in plenty or in want. I can do all this
through him who gives me strength" (Philippians 4:12, 13).

Paul gave a similar message to the Christians in Colossae: "Let the peace
of Christ rule in your hearts, since as members of one body you were called to
peace. And be thankful. Let the message of Christ dwell among you richly as you
teach and admonish one another with all wisdom through psalms, hymns, and
songs from the Spirit, singing to God with gratitude in your hearts" (Colossians
3:15, 16).

Adjusting our perception of the situation and of the perpetrator helps us
face reality and makes confronting the perpetrator more productive. Recognizing
and restoring appreciation for the intrinsic value of every person restores our
self-confidence, making confrontation less defensive and more helpful. Keeping
the good as well as the bad in view gives us confidence, hope, and peace, in
spite of the evil we experience. These broad categories point toward a number of
concrete and helpful suggestions that are common knowledge today.

Paul tells us the result of using these approaches: "As God's chosen people, holy and dearly loved, clothe yourselves with compassion, kindness, humility, gentleness and patience. Bear with each other and forgive one another if any of you has a grievance against someone. Forgive as the Lord forgave you. And over all these virtues put on love, which binds them all together in perfect unity" (verses 12–14).

In these verses Paul added a descriptor that both challenges and discourages me. "Forgive as the Lord forgave you," he said. What does that mean? How did Christ react to those who hurt Him? And how can I possibly live up to His divine example? That will be the focus of the next two chapters.

CHAPTER FIFTEEN

Rainy-Day Forgiveness

I am struck by the determination with which many of us human beings work at learning to do some things. Barbara and I took a nearly month-long trip with our daughter, son-in-law, and two preschool-aged grandchildren. I can't tell you how many times we heard a young voice calling out, "Look, Grandpa. See what I can do?" and "Grandma, did you know I could do this? Watch me! Watch me!" Most human beings want desperately to prove themselves capable. We avoid failure at all costs; and we minimize our shortcomings and emphasize the things we consider to be laudable accomplishments.

We see this dynamic at work in the political world. Acrimonious accusations fly, and those who disagree with some proposed project are labeled uncooperative, obstructionist, and irresponsible. Each side disparages every other viewpoint because each wants to be right.

Unfortunately, this isn't restricted to children and politicians. The story of Peter's betrayal of Jesus is a wonderful illustration of that. We can learn some good lessons from it, not just about our personal lives and relationships with other human beings, but some wonderful spiritual lessons as well.

The story begins in Mark 14:

"You will all fall away," Jesus told them [His disciples], "for it is written:

" 'I will strike the shepherd,
and the sheep will be scattered.'

"But after I have risen, I will go ahead of you into Galilee."

Peter declared, "Even if all fall away, I will not" (verses 27–29).

Human determination

I enjoy Peter. I hope my characterization of him and my assumptions about him aren't entirely false and that he wouldn't be too offended by my descriptions of him. I picture him as a rash, brash, impulsive, very determined, and quite accomplished person who jumped into the spotlight whenever anyone switched it on. He wanted to be in the center of the circle, right where everything was happening.

Recently, a story about an exceptionally brave man reminded me of Peter. This man knew no fear. He scaled rock cliffs without the protection of ropes or other safety apparatuses. He jumped out of airplanes at higher altitudes than anybody else did, and he waited longer than anybody else to open his parachute. He was a risk taker; a bold, in-your-face, "I'm going to show you what a human being can do" kind of person. I imagine that Peter would have lived that kind of irrational, risk-taking life.

Peter had objected to Jesus' statement that *all* the disciples would desert Him, saying that even if all the rest would desert Jesus, he would not. At this, Jesus specifically and pointedly warned Peter that before the rooster crowed twice—in other words, before dawn came again, he would disown Jesus three times. "But," Scripture says, "Peter insisted emphatically, 'Even if I have to die with you, I will never disown you' " (verse 31).

Absolutely confident in himself, Peter *knew* he could be faithful to Jesus. I would guess that very soon after this exchange with Jesus he began formulating ideas about how he could prove to Jesus that he could do what he said he would. Self-sufficiency was his mark. Proving oneself capable is a human characteristic.

Human effort

Not long after this, the mob came to Gethsemane to get Jesus. Peter was ready for them. In a flash he drew his dagger and attacked the first person he could reach: the high priest's servant. That man was fortunate that he hadn't lost his head! Peter had managed to sever only his ear.

How did Jesus respond to Peter's attempt to protect Him? Did He say, "Oh, thank you, Peter—I'm so glad you rescued Me. I don't know what I would have done without your help"?

No, that's *not* what Jesus said. Instead, He said something like, " 'No more of this!' And he touched the man's ear and healed him" (Luke 22:51).

Jesus rejected Peter's attempt to save Him. In fact, He turned Peter's approach to life upside down. Peter attacked, but Jesus yielded. Peter wounded, but Jesus healed.

What did Jesus want Peter to do, and what does He want us to do? Does He want a company of bystanders—people willing to observe but unwilling to engage themselves? People who stand by and let things happen; people who approach life passively rather than assertively intervening and working to improve? What role are we to fill in this world?

That question must have puzzled Peter. I wonder what was going through his mind as Jesus was taken into custody, as He was led down the Mount of Olives into the city and to the courtyard of the high priest. We do know that most of the other disciples ran away, just as Jesus had said they would. But Peter hadn't run away. He kept his promise not to desert Jesus.

As Peter followed the mob into the city, he must have decided that instead of confronting those who were holding Jesus, he would infiltrate their forces and by deception stay close to Jesus so that when the crisis came, he would be ready to act. He was determined to help Jesus one way or another.

That's funny, isn't it? The idea that the Creator of the universe would need a fisherman's help—even if that fisherman were brave, fairly capable, and very assertive. To think that God Himself would need the help of human beings is ludicrous, but I find that sometimes our thinking amounts to that.

Do we make room in our everyday lives for God to act? How? What risks do we take to allow God to intervene? In what ways can we see God's leading, and when we see that, do we follow Him rather than giving in to our own inclinations? What does God expect from us, and what will He do in our place, on our behalf?

As Peter waited with the others in the courtyard, several people began to probe his identity. I was in a similar situation a number of years ago. I was traveling in England at a time when America had a rather poor reputation among Europeans. So, to be frank about it, in that place and at that time I didn't want to be identified as an American. Consequently, while I was standing at a bus stop and visiting with a person from that area, I tried to assume a bit of a British accent. I wasn't sure how well I was doing until the person with whom I was talking asked me what part of England I was from. I was ecstatic. I was able to hide my identity. As I rode on the bus, I reveled in my accomplishment.

But when I got off the bus at my stop and headed down the street, a man tapped me on the shoulder and said, "Excuse me—what part of the States are you from?"

I was crestfallen. "How did you know I am an American?" I asked.

"I could tell by the way you walk," he replied.

We are who we are, aren't we? Peter did his best to hide his identity. No doubt he adjusted his clothes a little and tried to disguise his Galilean accent. And every time it got a little too hot at one fire pit, he moved to another—anything to cover up who he really was. But he had to face the reality that his attempts to hide his identity weren't working very well. The questioners became his nemesis. "Don't I remember seeing you somewhere before?" they said. "Weren't you one of those who followed this man?" "I'm sure I saw you with Jesus." "Aren't you the one who cut off my cousin's ear?" And before the cock did its crowing, Peter failed.

Confrontation didn't work; infiltration didn't work. And then Jesus—the bound prisoner, facing the most trying time of His life on earth—looked across the courtyard at arrogant, self-assured, cocky, confident Peter, and when their eyes met, Peter crumbled. The Bible doesn't tell us what he did then. In my imagination I see him stumbling away from that courtyard into the cool morning air with his eyes blurred with tears and his head bursting with rage and grief.

Peter staggers down Jerusalem's deserted streets, his arms flailing in gestures of despair. In one wild movement his hand slaps against his thigh, and instead of feeling the flesh of his leg, he feels hard metal—the knife that, the night before, Jesus had told him to put away. The knife is there. We don't know that Peter considered suicide, but it wouldn't be surprising, would it? Peter had failed to keep his promise. He had failed to protect his Master. He had betrayed the Lord. At that point he hated himself. No doubt he thought, *Since Jesus is going to die, why should I go on living? After what I've done, how can I live with myself?*

Our impulse in times of embarrassment and shame is to slink quietly away by ourselves, to avoid the reality of who we are, to hide our disgrace from eyes that now know us better than we ever wished to be known.

We can see that in children. We adults usually become relatively competent at disguising our true selves. But children who are corrected or reprimanded display both anger and shame at the same time. Using their anger to protect themselves from shame, they run away. They don't want anybody to touch them or hug them—they just want to be alone.

It seems reasonable to me to believe that Peter reacted that way that morning. In writhing anguish, he again and again plays through the scenes of those last hours: his confidence that he can hang on to his dream of Jesus's kingdom. His determination to make it happen. Jesus' calm prediction and its fulfillment. And the several ways in which his strategies had failed him. All those memories circle through his mind until he remembers Jesus' final instructions: "After I have risen, I will go ahead of you into Galilee" (Mark 14:28).

None of the disciples commented on those words at that time, but I wonder if the memory of what Jesus promised might not have been what brought Peter back from the despair of that cold morning into the circle of his friends and toward the embrace of his God. Jesus knew this was going to happen. He knew that Peter was going to desert Him. He knew that Peter couldn't do what he promised. Yet even though Jesus knew, He still wanted to be with Peter again.

Let that message sink into you. At your worst moment, Jesus wants to meet you. When you are most incapable, most ashamed, Jesus wants to be with you. That's good news, isn't it! Even before Jesus was betrayed, He graciously offered a way out and promised reinstatement.

Rainy-day forgiveness

You've heard about the wisdom of establishing a rainy-day fund—kind of a personal escrow account, if you will, that you set aside so you have something from which you can draw in times of financial crisis. Though you don't know when you'll need it, it'll be there whenever you do because you planned ahead. That's what Jesus was doing for Peter. He was making a deposit of rainy-day forgiveness—forgiveness ahead of time. It's a stunning statement of the grace of the One who was betrayed, of forgiveness from the One who was wronged. It's a promise of God's great provision in advance for the time when it will be needed most.

"After I have risen, I will go ahead of you into Galilee." When Jesus said this, He knew what was ahead. He knew that Peter would need that promise—that it would be his lifeline to the future.

John 21 tells us what happened when Jesus met Peter in Galilee. The first part of that chapter pictures a crew of frustrated fishermen. After a period of disappointment and despair in Jerusalem, they had gone back to their homes. Those who had fished on Lake Galilee returned to their fishing. All night long they were on the water. (There were no laws against night fishing at that time!) When the sky began to lighten, they headed toward the shore. Someone there—a shadowy figure of a person whom they couldn't identify because of the distance—called out to them, "Do you have any fish?"

"No," they shouted back. "We worked all night and didn't catch anything."

"Well," said the backseat driver on the shore, "throw your net on the other side of the boat."

Think about the humor of that crazy suggestion—as if fish swimming in the unfenced underwater world paid attention to which side of the boat they were on! It made no sense, yet there was something in the command that prompted the disciples to do what the stranger said.

The result? Their nets were overloaded with fish. The disciples recognized that this was a miracle—which likely meant that Jesus was there.

The moment that Peter realized who the stranger on the shore was, he jumped out of the boat and swam toward shore. And when those who had stayed on the boat got to shore, Jesus fed all of them breakfast. He addressed their human needs by providing fish for their needs and for the needs of their families. Then Jesus engaged Peter in a spiritual conversation.

> When they had finished eating, Jesus said to Simon Peter, "Simon son of John, do you truly love me more than these?"
>
> "Yes, Lord," he said, "you know that I love you."
>
> Jesus said, "Feed my lambs."
>
> Again Jesus said, "Simon son of John, do you love me?"
>
> He answered, "Yes, Lord, you know that I love you."
>
> Jesus said, "Take care of my sheep."
>
> The third time he said to him, "Simon son of John, do you love me?"

Peter was hurt because Jesus asked him the third time, "Do you love me?" He said, "Lord, you know all things; you know that I love you."

Jesus said, "Feed my sheep" (John 21:15–17).

John, the disciple we sometimes think of as being the most emotional, the most sensitive one of the group, tells this story. Aware of the dynamics in the relationship between Jesus and Peter, John says that Jesus asked Peter whether he loved Him more than did the other disciples. I wish we had a recording of that conversation—I'd like to hear the tone of Peter's voice when he answered Jesus' questions.

Had I been in Peter's place, I would have wanted to avoid that discussion. I would have wished those bad memories had been buried forever. I would have wished someone had just let them go away. If I had been the one whom Jesus was questioning, I would have been hoping that nobody else would hear my response, and I would have answered as quickly and as quietly as I could, "You know that I love You."

"Feed my lambs." Ah—the sheep thing now comes up again. Perhaps Jesus meant something like, "Like sheep, all of you will scatter. You, Peter, take care of the lambs—the little, vulnerable, cute ones; the ones you love being with; those that energize and delight you. Take care of them for me."

Eventually—and who knows how long the pause is—Jesus asks again, "Simon, son of John, do you love me?"

Oh no—not again! Perhaps Peter thought, *Maybe Jesus didn't hear me the first time.* So he answers again, "Yes, Lord, you know that I love you."

At Peter's response, Jesus replies, "Take care of my sheep." Not just the cute little ones, the babies. Now it's "Take care of my sheep."

I don't know much about sheep. I've had only one experience directly with them. I was visiting a friend on a farm, and we went out into a mountain meadow where sheep were grazing. I didn't realize that the ram didn't like strangers until he started after me. Fortunately, there were stumps standing in the meadow, remnants of the clearing homesteaders had done decades earlier. My only refuge was on top of one of those stumps. I had to climb onto it and hope someone would rescue me!

"Feed my sheep." Sheep can be obnoxious. They don't take instructions well.

You can't teach them much. And it's hard to get them to go where they're supposed to go. Sheep can be annoying. But Jesus says, "Feed my sheep."

There's a pause, and then a third time Jesus asks, "Simon, son of John, do you love me?"

Here the writer of this Gospel opens our eyes and hearts and says that Peter was hurt that Jesus would ask him the third time, "Do you love me?" That calloused, tough, "do it no matter what the obstacles are" person; that determined, successful man was hurt because Jesus confronted him with his true identity.

"Lord," Peter says, "You know all things. You know me. You know how rash and impulsive and quick tempered I am. You know how disloyal I can be."

What phrases would you, the reader, use here if you were to quietly and privately describe yourself? Would you say something like "You know how easily I forget the lessons I learn. You know how prone I am to succumb to temptation. You know all things, which means that You know me. So You know that I love You."

Jesus again tells Peter, "Feed my sheep." Jesus directs Peter to reengage in the work to which He had called him. He invites Peter back from his despair into the circle of active disciples. He wishes for Peter a renewed sense of purpose and mission. He reclaims Peter from shame and defeat and makes his life meaningful again.

This story shows us how Jesus deals with people who fail. He meets them on the shore of their unsuccessful fishing trip. He welcomes them back after their failure. He helps them find success, and He loves them in spite of themselves.

What does Jesus do with the guilty? He relates to them much as He does to those who fail. He claims as His the people who hate themselves. He accepts those who betray Him. He restores the unworthy and reinstates the alienated. He gently warns of failure and promises forgiveness anyway.

God hasn't limited Himself to Peter. His mercy is available to you and to me today and tomorrow and next week and next month. On our rainy days, you and I can benefit from God's gifts of forgiveness and love. Nothing we've done can keep God from forgiving us. In fact, He already has a supply of forgiveness all stored up just for our emergencies. Think of it: God's grace-filled gift is provided in advance for every crisis you and I face.

Rainy-day forgiveness—forgiveness that God has stocked up ahead of time so it's available to us whenever we need it. Isn't that great news!

CHAPTER SIXTEEN

Forgiving Ourselves

As I write this chapter, the university where I work is preparing to celebrate the graduation of the students who have met the requirements for the degrees they will receive. They are elated and feel successful. They have accomplished something significant, and that bolsters their self-esteem. But to those who failed a required class or haven't completed a required project—well, these are not happy days. Those students probably are troubled by doubts about themselves. They probably are struggling with, as we term it, "low self-worth."

Our performance is a very fragile foundation on which to build our self-worth. We all fail to live up to our expectations for ourselves. We all say and do things that we later regret, and our failures can haunt us for years. As long as we measure our worth by what we *do,* we're bound to feel disappointed in ourselves, and guilty, and even worthless. So it isn't surprising that people often ask me how they can forgive themselves.

For example, consider how an addict feels when she has promised herself and those she loves that she'll never again use her drug of choice, but then, despite her determination, and despite her success for days and weeks and maybe even months, she succumbs to the temptation again. Her resistance to it had made her feel good about herself—proud of her accomplishments. They had increased her self-esteem. Now she doubts she can ever change. And those who had come to believe that she was going to be successful this time lose all hope for her. How can she forgive herself?

Consider too the man who can't control his temper but who feels ashamed of himself after each episode of violence. He promises his battered wife that if she will give him another chance, he won't hurt her again. But then, after months of living up to his promise, he does it again—and this time his wife goes to the emergency room, tells the truth about what happened to her, and files a restraining order to protect herself and their children from him. The loss of his family, his embarrassment, and his regret weigh on him, and he feels horrible. How can he ever forgive himself?

Our choices

What choices do people have in these circumstances? They can pretend that they've done nothing wrong and deny that they have a problem. Some try that, saying they only drink socially or use drugs recreationally or that those whom they've hurt deserved what they did to them. But those who bury the truth about themselves either are lying deliberately or are so far out of touch with reality as to render themselves truly helpless.

The better alternative is for us to accept our responsibility and admit our failure. But for those whose self-esteem is fragile, this option seems devastating. They've worked hard to prove their worth because they believe that's the way to earn acceptance and affirmation and love. The counsel that they must admit to being failures floors them, and they become empty husks, despondent and listless.

So, when people ask how they can they forgive themselves, I tell them, they can't—not if they're going to be honest. The Bible says, "All have sinned and fall short of the glory of God" (Romans 3:23).

That doesn't sound good. But it isn't the bad news that it appears to be. In fact, it's at this declaration, at this admission of the truth, that forgiveness begins. While people can't forgive themselves, the astonishingly good news is that God offers to forgive them. As Paul put it, "At just the right time, when we were still powerless, Christ died for the ungodly. Very rarely will anyone die for a righteous person, though for a good person someone might possibly dare to die. But God demonstrates his own love for us in this: While we were still sinners, Christ died for us" (Romans 5:6–8).

God's love for us differs markedly from the kind of love we receive from ourselves and other people. Instead of conditioning His love on how well we

perform, God loves us *in spite of our performance!* We don't earn His affirmation—
He gives it to us before we've done anything to deserve it! His is the gold standard
of unconditional acceptance, and it is based on who we are rather than on what
we do. Scripture says that to all who received Him, "to those who believed in
his name, he gave the right to become children of God—children born not of
natural descent, nor of human decision or a husband's will, but born of God"
(John 1:12, 13).

The good news is that God has claimed us as His in spite of our failures.
He proclaims us to be His heirs, descendants of His according to His promise,
because of our acceptance of Christ! (See Galatians 3:29.) God has offered us
forgiveness, and, through Christ, has overcome our failures. "All this is from
God, who reconciled us to himself through Christ and gave us the ministry
of reconciliation: that God was reconciling the world to himself in Christ, not
counting people's sins against them" (2 Corinthians 5:18, 19).

The humbling yet freeing truth is that God has done all this on His own.
That we are guilty and feel ashamed doesn't matter. What God has offered us
doesn't depend on our being successful. God loves us for *who we are* without
any requirement other than that we trust Him. "God so loved the world that he
gave his one and only Son, that whoever believes in him shall not perish but have
eternal life. For God did not send his Son into the world to condemn the world,
but to save the world through him. Whoever believes in him is not condemned"
(John 3:16–18).

No condemnation. What a powerful statement that is! Even when we're feeling our greatest regret, God doesn't condemn us. Even then He stands by us.
And,

> If God is for us, who can be against us? He who did not spare
> his own Son, but gave him up for us all—how will he not also,
> along with him, graciously give us all things? Who will bring any
> charge against those whom God has chosen? It is God who jus-
> tifies. Who then is the one who condemns? No one. Christ Jesus
> who died—more than that, who was raised to life—is at the right
> hand of God and is also interceding for us. Who shall separate us
> from the love of Christ? Shall trouble or hardship or persecution
> or famine or nakedness or danger or sword? As it is written:

"For your sake we face death all day long;
we are considered as sheep to be slaughtered."

No, in all these things we are more than conquerors through him who loved us. For I am convinced that neither death nor life, neither angels nor demons, neither the present nor the future, nor any powers, neither height nor depth, nor anything else in all creation, will be able to separate us from the love of God that is in Christ Jesus our Lord (Romans 8:31–39).

We can't forgive ourselves—but that doesn't mean that we must feel we have no worth. Real worth lies in the value others regard us as having. The Creator God forever established our value when He sacrificed Himself for us. That you are supremely valuable is clear because God paid the supreme price for you!

The point is . . .

Johnny Lingo, a short movie produced by the Latter-day Saints in 1969, portrays the effect that people's valuations of others have upon them. The story is set on one of the islands of Polynesia. Mahana, a girl who lives there, is so sullen and ugly that her neighbors and even her family think her to be so undesirable that no one will want to marry her.

Then Johnny Lingo, a successful trader, comes to this island to bargain for a wife. The custom is that a man wishing to marry pays the father of the prospective bride in cows—and of course, the more valuable the bride is, the more cows the groom must give her father. Mahana's neighbors wonder whether Johnny will give her father even one cow for her.

The man who's overseeing the bargaining session suggests that Mahana's father start it by asking Johnny for three cows. At this the neighbors all laugh, thinking he'll be lucky if he gets one. But Johnny says that while three cows is a lot, Mahana is worth much more. He says he'll give Mahana's father eight cows for her. Mahana's father, of course, agrees. So Johnny and Mahana marry, and then they leave on a trading trip.

Here's the point of the movie: when Johnny and Mahana return from their trip, the islanders are astounded at the transformation that has taken place. Sullen, ugly Mahana has become a beautiful and happy woman—all because Johnny treated her as being of great worth, of great value.

God paid the supreme price for us. By doing so He has shown how much He cares for us. We haven't earned that valuation. We can only accept or reject it.

Similarly, we can't forgive ourselves, but we can have forgiveness because God offers it to us. We don't need to do anything to earn the forgiveness He offers us. All He asks is that we believe that He has already provided all we need. The real issue isn't whether we can prove our worth, but whether we will trust God and accept His affirmation of us.

This is the same test Adam and Eve faced. Would they believe what God said, or would they instead believe what they saw and heard from the serpent? Would they trust what God promised—that their lives would be long and productive if they ate the fruit produced by the tree of life—or would they try to make themselves wise by eating the fruit that came from the tree of knowledge of good and evil? Would they trust what God provided, or would they try to take care of themselves?

We can't forgive ourselves, but we can believe that God has already forgiven us, and we can rest peacefully and confidently in His love and care.

CHAPTER SEVENTEEN

The Miracle Solution

In chapter 8 of this book I tell how the murder of our daughter affected me spiritually. At first, my primary emotion was sadness. That morphed into a depression that felt like an emotionless void. And then, as the anniversary of Shannon's death approached, anger began to make its presence known. At first, it appeared spasmodically, but then it began to grow and deepen until it was on the verge of overwhelming me. I tried to do everything that's supposed to help us reduce the load of stress we carry, but neither the secular practices nor the spiritual ones did the job.

Then one Sabbath, John Cress preached a sermon on Jesus' instruction that we are to love one another. That brought to my mind the even more challenging mandate Jesus has given us that we are to love our enemies. I had tried to forgive Anthony, but I couldn't do it—and that brought into question my spiritual standing. How could I be a Christian—let alone a pastor, a chaplain, a teacher of religion in a Christian college—when I couldn't do one of the most basic things that Jesus asked of His followers? I realized that it wasn't just a matter of changing my actions; I needed to change on the inside. I was as much in need of God's transforming grace and as incapable of changing the reality of who I am as was Anthony—Shannon's murderer—in his cell in Maryland.

I was devastated! But it wasn't my words and acts that troubled me most; it was the shame of who I was. I wasn't as concerned about humiliating public exposure as I was about the inner pain. I didn't care what others saw or knew about me; it was the truth about me that crushed me. That was much more horrible than having others see my failures.

So, the words of Paul echoed in my mind: "What a wretched man I am! Who will rescue me from this body that is subject to death?" (Romans 7:24).

Paul's cry of desperation

Countless numbers of us have echoed the cry of desperation Paul voiced. Who can deliver us from this body that is subject to death? Who can save us from the truth about ourselves? Who can make successes of us when we've failed—make us reliable carriers of forgiveness when we're filled with resentment?

Who can save us from ourselves?

Fortunately, Paul pointed toward the answer to his question. He wrote, "Thanks be to God, who delivers me through Jesus Christ our Lord!" (verse 25).

God identifies the most neglected aspect—which also happens to be the most essential aspect—of becoming forgiving people. It is the turbobooster of the forgiveness process—the ultimate solution for the tough cases that we can't solve by what we can do for ourselves. It goes beyond applying our minds and hearts to our situation. God Himself delivers us from this body that is subject to death (see verse 24) *by changing us.* As helpful as these other approaches are, they change only our feelings or our behavior; they don't change *us.* God, however, *does* change us. He transforms our nature—and in doing so makes us new creatures who can do what we couldn't do before. When we are transformed, not only can we forgive a hurtful word or a sinful act, but we become forgiving people.

For the most part, we live in a concrete world, but sin is an abstraction. We respond to a world that we can see and hear and touch and taste; a world of senses and feelings, and we focus on specific incidents—on "sins"—because they are part of this concrete world. They are individual thoughts, words, or acts that hurt and damage other people. Sins leave in their train the pain of broken relationships and the devastation of shattered self-esteem. Even when the sins are committed by someone else and are directed against us, we carry them with us. We carry the perpetrator's abuses or betrayals.

Often, those who are wounded by the sins of others can find relief for their suffering by following the processes outlined in the preceding chapters of this book and what other people have found to be helpful. However, we, too, easily neglect or ignore the "sin" that produces these "sins." The sin that functions at a deeper level. The sin that is the root cause of all human misery. Sin is a fundamental isolation from the goodness of God and from the best of ourselves. It is a permeating evil that wreaks havoc on others and on us. Often, we are slow to recognize and acknowledge that it is sin that lies behind most of the troubles we endure.

When we try to forgive those who have sinned against us, we tend to target "sins." But, curiously, our success poses a danger to us. When we successfully eliminate sins, we're tempted to forget what causes them. This is a danger especially to those who have no religious faith and who don't think of the relationship between God and humanity. Their naturalistic beliefs about how human beings function and their prescriptions of ways to achieve forgiveness on the human level pose the danger of ending the symptoms without eliminating the disease. Those methods *do* work. They *do* bring relief. Many of the principles and instructions they contain harmonize with those we find in the Bible. But unless we complement our efforts to eliminate these symptoms with an attack on the root cause of the problem, we will never become whole.

We would question a friend who treated her smoker's cough by taking cough suppressant while continuing to smoke, or a son who keeps adding oil to an engine that needs a ring job, or a cook who discards the burned toast but doesn't turn down the toaster. However, we do much the same thing if we always deal with sins but never with sin. We might be able to eliminate what's distressing us now, but that doesn't mean we've solved the real problem. One can forgive a specific instance of sin without becoming a forgiving person. Yet until we become forgiving persons, we'll always have to struggle with offenses.

We need to deal both with sins and with sin. And we need to forgive the sins others commit against us and to seek forgiveness for the sins we commit against other people. We need both to forgive and to be forgiven.

Fortunately, God will help us with both!

Victims, not the guilty

Let's be clear though. This view of our nature doesn't mean that victims of attacks bear some responsibility for those attacks and therefore we shouldn't grieve when someone has attacked us because our sinful nature makes us guilty too.

The need to be forgiven differs from our willingness to forgive someone who has hurt us in some way. No matter how disobedient or irritating children may be, they aren't responsible for the sin adults commit when they lose their tempers and abuse them. Nor is the guilt of those who commit sexual assaults lessened because their victims were sexually provocative. Recognizing our inherent guilt doesn't neutralize the consequences for perpetrators. It may be necessary to separate yourself and this discussion from the specific instance for which you wish to forgive another in order for you to make this distinction.

We are talking here about the *state* of sin more than just sinful *acts*. That we are guilty on both accounts is certainly true. Even the best of us do bad things and are thus guilty of sinful acts. But accepting forgiveness for our misdeeds—which some people label "forgiving ourselves"—differs from being forgiven for who we are at the core of ourselves.* The first involves external behaviors or individual offenses. The second involves our very selves—our identity, who we are.

The cumulative impact produced by the human race's separation of itself from God since the time of Adam and Eve affects all of us. This state of moral and physical degeneracy has become the launching pad of our individual choices. Each of us is inherently attracted toward self and away from God. We tend to take rather than to give. We admire those who accumulate more than they need. This condition defines our corporate and individual guilt and our need for forgiveness. That forgiveness comes only from God, and it comes as a spiritual experience rather than by human effort.

We begin to experience God's forgiveness when we face the reality about ourselves. For me, that happened in church, when I realized I couldn't make myself be the person I wanted to be. I was a desperate failure at following Christ's command that I love my enemy, and that devastated me. Never before had I felt so far from God, nor had I ever been so aware of my helplessness.

Initially, that face-off with reality produced an overwhelming sense of despair. But then I remembered the assurance Paul gave us that Christ died for the ungodly; that He died for us while we were still sinners (Romans 5:6). It seemed to me that Paul wrote those words just for me! At what I thought to be the most desperate moment of my life, those words confronted me with the startling

---

* "Forgiving ourselves" strikes me as being a misnomer. We don't forgive either the one we offended or God or ourselves. It is only the victim of the offense who forgives; the offender certainly doesn't have the standing to forgive himself or herself.

reality of Jesus' love. He knew what would happen to me at this stage of my life, so He died to rescue me from myself!

The thought that God cared for me when I saw myself as worthless; the realization that even then He was thinking of me and reaching out to me overwhelmed me. The depth of my despair—more profound than anything I had felt at any other point in my life—was satiated by the inexhaustible supply of God's grace, and I haven't been the same since. The bouts I fought with guilt have ended since I realized that if God loved me in spite of this profound, intrinsic flaw of mine, He can easily stay by me through the failures that it generates.

Experiencing God's forgiveness has changed my view of myself. It performed another stunning miracle for me too. As we walked out of church that day, I realized that another long-held hurt had disappeared. Without any indication that the offender had changed or that I had misunderstood, the burden I had carried since the day of Shannon's death was gone. There had been no reconciliation, but the pain was gone. I no longer felt chained to that experience. A huge relief lifted me from the doldrums of anger and resentment into the peaceful reality of becoming a forgiving person. That was a miracle!

Since that day, other people have shared with me their stories of similar journeys. They, too, had been sick at heart and filled with resentment. They, too, had experienced a healing confrontation with Jesus that ended when they had a clear view of their nature. That perspective changed their reality even though the circumstances hadn't changed. In some cases there was a reconciliation; in most, there wasn't any. But everyone experienced relief, which they attributed to God. It was God's gift and not their accomplishment. They were confronted by their own sin; they grieved and regretted the sin at the core of their being; and then they experienced God's forgiveness—at which point their resentment and hatred disappeared, and they no longer desired revenge.

A biblical pattern

What happened to them and to me followed a pattern described in Scripture. The first step is our becoming aware of reality. Both by nature and by individual choice we stand isolated from God, the Life-Giver. As Paul put it: "All have sinned and fall short of the glory of God" (Romans 3:23).

From the beginning, God signaled His intention to heal that rift by sending Jesus to be our Savior. "God so loved the world that he gave his one and only Son, that whoever believes in him shall not perish but have eternal life" (John 3:16).

Soon after Jesus' resurrection and ascension, Peter stood before the Sanhedrin. In reply to their questioning, he described Jesus' crucial role in God's plan to save human beings. He said of the resurrected Christ, "God exalted him to his own right hand as Prince and Savior that he might bring Israel to repentance and forgive their sins" (Acts 5:31).

So God initiated both repentance and forgiveness. Both were gifts given by the resurrected Lord.

In the next verse Peter described the natural result of being forgiven—forgiveness gives rise to "witnessing" about one's experience to others. Peter wrote, "We are witnesses of these things, and so is the Holy Spirit, whom God has given to those who obey him" (Acts 5:32).

It seems clear from the context that here *witnessing* means more than simply observing something. When Peter and the other disciples were taken into custody, they were talking about what they had seen. They were telling the others about their experiences. Not at all limited to a silent viewing of the forgiveness event, they were telling to anyone who would listen what it did for them.

Jesus made several post-Resurrection appearances to the disciples. Luke, in his Gospel, records Jesus picturing the same sequence that the other disciples wrote about. "This is what is written: The Messiah will suffer and rise from the dead on the third day, and repentance for the forgiveness of sins will be preached in his name to all nations, beginning at Jerusalem. You are witnesses of these things" (Luke 24:46–48).

It appears that in his speech to the Sanhedrin, Peter was simply repeating the words of Jesus. Repentance and forgiveness are inseparably connected with Jesus, and experiencing the wonderful relief that comes from repentance and forgiveness leads us to share our good news with others. The whole experience transforms those who go through it. Our anger and resentment are taken away, and we no longer loathe the perpetrator. We no longer want to punish him or her. And when we've been forgiven, we became more tolerant of others without even trying. This is indeed a miracle!

That we, as human beings, were taking steps toward forgiveness doesn't mean that God had nothing to do with it. I object to defining a miracle as something we can't do ourselves or that we can't explain. Picturing God as confined to the holes in reality—the things we don't understand—restricts Him to smaller and smaller parts of human experience. In that case it's true that the more that science and psychology progress, the less we need God. In fact, there are those who say we no longer need God at all since we understand our natures so well and take such good care of ourselves. They claim that people use God as a crutch, and that He's primarily a way for us to escape responsibility for our own inaction or willful ignorance. They define God as the opiate of the masses. They say that the One upon whom we relied in our primitive state is dead, or that God is no longer closely involved in our existence.

I prefer to recognize a God who surprises us and changes us. The God described in Scripture repeatedly intervened in human events to bring temporary relief and eternal hope. God works through natural as well as supernatural processes, so I stretch the meaning of *miracle* to include what we understand as awesome as well as what we don't understand at all.

So, in addition to empowering the steps we take toward the forgiveness of sins, God provides divine relief from the burden of sin. He accepts us despite our having sinful natures, and He doesn't say that we must work for it or we must reach a certain spiritual level if we desire to be forgiven. It's true that implementing the steps of forgiveness requires effort, discipline, and determination on our part. But experiencing God's forgiveness of us in spite of who we are results from God's work, not ours. God acts, and we accept what He offers us. We open our hands and exchange the burden we were carrying for God's solution. We let God's efforts take effect in us, and what He does is a miracle!

Until we experience the depth of God's love for us and His desire to forgive us, we cannot adequately forgive and love others. But once we experience God's love, we will respond to it by loving and forgiving others. This makes the concept and application of love crucially important to the process of forgiving, and it explains why the essays that follow are so useful.

PART THREE

Attitude Change:
Essays on Love

CHAPTER EIGHTEEN

Introduction

The following reflections provide the background and foundation for a healthy and workable experience of forgiveness. They address the following issues: self-esteem that allows us to forgive ourselves, anger that blocks us from forgiving others, and criticism that is a key to growth and improvement. They emphasize that God expects us to love ourselves, and they call us to love others. They suggest that we make a clear distinction between the person himself or herself on the one hand, and, on the other, what that person thinks or does or says. They encourage us to replace our resentment and anger toward others with an attitude of love.

The original author, Frank Kimper, was a United Methodist minister with specialized education and training as a pastoral counselor. For years he taught pastoral counseling at the School of Theology in Claremont, California, where I was his student. A warm, accepting, and honest mentor, he endeared himself to me and to many others by living out the principles of love and acceptance that he taught.

Kimper's approach addresses the needs of both victims and perpetrators. It offers a tangible way for victims to reorient their view of the trauma they suffered and of the perpetrators who caused that trauma. His approach provides a framework in which perpetrators can be held accountable for what they have done yet also be recognized as persons of worth. It frees survivors from the burden of resentment and the quest for revenge. It provides a way to reclaim or strengthen their self-esteem while preserving an atmosphere that encourages critique and evaluation, both of which are crucial to the learning and growth of both perpetrators and victims. Here you'll find a realistic way to actualize the often-repeated dictum "hate the sin, but love the sinner."

The symptoms of disharmony in human relations are many and varied, but the root cause seems always to be the same: an unwillingness to love—to see another human being as precious and to allow that attitude to predominate in everyday living. This is tough—a strait gate and a narrow way. But it is the way to a contented and happy life.

What follows are a few essays that are part of an extensive series. As Kimper's understanding of Scripture, theology, and psychology grew, he revised and re-wrote his essays from time to time—adding illustrations and tweaking them to fit new insights or to make them more relevant.

Kimper copied and distributed various forms of these reflections to students and friends, but he never published them. All Scripture references are his own paraphrases. They are both delightfully relevant and contemporary while also being consistent with the intent of the original passage. The structure that follows and the basic ideas are his, too, but I have radically reworded and edited some of them.

It is my hope that as you read and contemplate what follows, you will experience the profound and personal impact of his ideas as I have.

CHAPTER NINETEEN

Love

Summary: True love recognizes and accepts the individual worth of every person.

One attitude is always present in a mature person, in a mature relationship, and in a mature society. That attitude is *love,* which I here define as respect for and recognition of the human worth of every person. Being loved means being respected as an individual and being appreciated as a person of value. Being loved in this way allows a person to live a contented life and enjoy fulfilling relationships. It is an essential ingredient to an ideal society.

All good relationships are founded on this attitude, and when it is missing or withheld, we feel hurt and/or angry. It is the one common element in all the great living religions and the one common element in all the major approaches to psychotherapy. It is a truth that does not need to be defended because, when practiced, experience itself validates it.

I hope you will allow these reflections to speak to you until you grasp this understanding of the meaning of love, or better yet, until this concept of love *as an attitude* grasps you. Then, seriously seek to maintain that attitude in your everyday experience with others. This is not an easy assignment, and you will never do it perfectly. But to whatever degree you do succeed, you will find it rewarding. I believe it is *the way* to become a forgiving person and that, in turn, is the way to a life of joy.

CHAPTER TWENTY

Affirmation

Summary: As every person is God's creation, God presumes that each one will recognize and accept his or her supreme worth and the supreme and equal worth of every other person. To do so is to love unconditionally.

An expert in the interpretation of Scripture asked Jesus, "What must I do to experience abundant life?"

Jesus replied, "You tell Me!"

The Scripture expert answered, "You must love God with all your heart and mind and soul and strength; and your neighbor as yourself."

Jesus commented, "Do that, and you will live."

This Scripture does not say you must love yourself. Rather, it assumes that you already do love yourself and that your love of yourself is an appropriate measure for your love of your neighbor and of God.

The fact is that I do love myself. The self I am is precious to me, because the self I am *is* me.

Misidentification: Who am I?

My true self is *not* my *body;* but I use my body to be myself.

My true self is *not* my *intelligence;* but I use my intelligence to consider and express myself.

My true self is *not* my *abilities;* but I use my abilities to make every form of self-expression as productive as my development of them will permit.

My true self is *not* my *appearance,* my *performance,* or my *accomplishments.* These are more the result of my abilities and opportunities than an expression of who I am.

Identity versus expression

I *love* (think "respect" and "value") the person I am. I *use* the capabilities I have at my disposal to express who I am.

My "self" is *equal* in worth to the self you are. The capabilities I have available to me are *unequal,* in strength and capacity, to the capabilities available to you.

To love you, my neighbor, is to perceive the person you are to be of *equal value* to the person I am.

Love *is not* . . .

Love is not a response to a body; otherwise, persons with unhealthy, unshapely bodies would get little or no love.

Love is not a response to intelligence; otherwise, persons with moronic or demonic minds would get little or no love.

Love is not a response to talent; otherwise, one-talent persons would get little or no love.

Love is not a response to appearance, performance, or products; otherwise, persons with mediocre capabilities and only slight opportunity for their development and use would get little or no love.

Love *is* . . .

Love is my perception of you as a precious person no matter what capabilities you have or how you use them. Body, mind, talents, and performance determine only the means by which we relate to others; *love* is the *attitude* in which we relate.

For me to love you and for you to love me as we love ourselves, we must love God with all our heart, mind, soul, and strength. But all self-expression is imperfect, so all loving is also imperfect—except one's love of self; one's respect for and valuing of one's self. That's an inherent recognition of the value God has placed on each of us and is a divine assumption.

CHAPTER TWENTY-ONE

Differences

Summary: Each person naturally strives to be and to express the unique and valuable person she or he is. Each has a God-given right to freely express that individuality, but that expression has consequences. Living harmoniously with others requires either adjusting personal preferences to the will of the group or receiving the consequences of disruptive and destructive choices.

I love you. This means "I perceive you to be precious," no matter what kind of body you may have, no matter what kind of mind you may have, no matter what abilities you may have, and no matter what kind of performance you put on. Actually, none of these has anything to do with the fact—and it is a fact—that you are precious. You are precious simply because you exist, whatever your capabilities and however you may use them. You were born that way. To see that and to be grasped by the reality of it is to love.

Among the fundamental characteristics of each person is an inherent thrust toward individuality. Believers in a Creator-God acknowledge each person as God's creation. Each one yearns to be recognized as separate and distinct and seeks the freedom to choose how and when and where to express their individuality. To love another means to recognize and acknowledge their uniqueness and their need and right to express themselves authentically.

Most babies like to be cuddled. They naturally seek inclusion in community. Soon after birth being swaddled comforts them, but as they grow, they seek more and more freedom to move. As toddlers, they begin to venture away from and then return to a trusted adult. If you restrict their movements so they cannot express themselves as they choose, they will become angry and fight to get out of your grip. If you frustrate them long enough, they will cry hot angry tears—their spontaneous reaction to their perception of a threat to their being *free*. Being free is precious.

But, of course, the unrestrained expression of freedom is quite impractical, because if everyone always did whatever they felt like doing, the result would be utter chaos and unbearable pain. Though the universe always scrupulously honors one's freedom, the principle of cause and effect functions with immediacy and precision to indicate which expressions of freedom are tolerable and which are not. A paraphrase of a biblical thought expresses this very well: God always offers us options—blessing or cursing, life or death, joy or pain. So choose for yourselves. *Choose for yourselves!* This is crucial. Freedom is perceived and honored as priceless, and no limitations are placed upon one's exercise of freedom as a condition for being loved. But obvious limitations are placed on one's exercise of freedom as conditions for living in the universe if one wants a healthy, happy, and satisfying life.

For instance, a thirty-nine-year-old mother of two teenagers was buried because the universe could no longer tolerate the combination of drugs and alcohol she chose to take into her body. Her being free was perceived and honored as precious, but the consequences of her use of that freedom demonstrated limits she chose to ignore.

Another young mother is grieving. Her eight-year-old daughter was "having fun" playing in the rain under a big oak tree. There was a flash of lightning, and the girl was killed. Her bereaved mother admits she approved the "fun" against her better judgment, and she feels terribly guilty about that. But she says, "I was afraid she would think I was just a 'mean mommy' if I didn't agree to let her go. Anyway, it was only drizzling, and I didn't think it was really dangerous."

The assumption is that wiser choices would result in health and joy, but it's a fact that because we are finite, we are never exactly sure what choice *is* wiser. So, every choice involves some risk. But it is a fact that we do have choices and that we often knowingly exercise our freedom in ways that the universe will barely tolerate. Paul put this in the context of interpersonal experience when he said to the Galatians:

> Brothers and sisters, we have the precious gift of freedom, only
> we are never really free to do just as we please. Jesus' summary of

the law, "Love your neighbor as yourself," directs us to exercise our freedom to express love. Yet it is equally possible to prey on each other in hateful ways.

To express love or hate: these are the choices before us, and the consequences are obvious. If we use our freedom to express hate, the results are quarrels, jealousy, murder, war, and the like. On the other hand, the results of using our freedom to express love are joy, peace, and goodwill. Make no mistake about it: each of us is personally responsible for our own use of it; and each will reap just what he or she sows. Those who sow hate will reap destruction, and those who sow love will reap abundant life (paraphrased from Galatians 5 and 6).

Like the laws of gravity, the law "Love your neighbor as yourself" has the authority of the universe behind it. Its command is clear, and the results, inevitable. To achieve satisfaction in interpersonal relations, you must exercise your freedom so as to give expression only to those forms of behavior that affirm others to be as precious as you know yourself to be. The consequence of obedience is a satisfying interpersonal experience. The consequence of disobedience is interpersonal conflict and pain.

This is the foundation for morality in interpersonal living. The efforts of human beings to respond to that command through the centuries have resulted in the formalizing of taboos, ethical practices, moral customs, bills of rights, and codes of law—all of which represent human attempts to spell out guidelines for the exercise of freedom so that every person would be *equally affirmed* as *equally precious*. This law defines the condition for living harmoniously with each other in family, school, work, community, national, and international relationships.

Kimper illustrations

When I was about twelve years old, I met Ray, a college student whose folks had just moved into our community. Ray commuted the twenty-five miles to Philadelphia to attend Drexel Institute, but he was home weekends, when a number of us kids didn't seem to know what to do with ourselves. Being a natural leader of boys, Ray would organize pickup games of baseball, football, or basketball, in season, to occupy a Saturday or a Sunday afternoon. Or he'd take us on a hike.

Many things about my relationship with Ray at that time profoundly affected my life. One was the fact that with respect to the rules of the game, he was impartial—there were no favorites. He also was strict—I often thought much too strict. But for him, rules were made to be kept, and they applied equally to everyone. Actually, I had to learn this the hard way, because I assumed, falsely, that my being a little squirt would justify my getting special privileges. I soon learned that being little got me no special favors and that the rules spelled out the conditions for our living together whether we were on the football field or on the basketball court.

I remember very clearly a pickup basketball game that Ray was refereeing, in which he said I fouled a guy. I didn't think I'd fouled that guy, and the call made me angry. I called Ray all kinds of names—cutting and cruel names. But he told me calmly that if I wouldn't play by the rules, I'd have to leave the game. This only made me angrier. I was seething with hate as we lined up for that foul shot. Impulsively, I tried to trip the opposing player who was standing next to me on the foul line by putting my foot in front of him. There was no doubt about what was in my mind. Ray saw what I had done, called another foul on me even before the first penalty shots were taken, and threw me out of the game. Furthermore, he told me I wouldn't be allowed to play again until I was willing to play by the rules.

I went home determined never to have anything more to do with Ray or with any of the boys. I wasn't going to have them telling me what I could and couldn't do. They let me hold my grudge without retaliating—but even more important, without making any concession whatever.

For several weeks—the most miserable weeks I had ever known—I knew I was only cheating myself, but I wouldn't admit I was wrong until finally, in spite of a feeling of awful humiliation, I told Ray I wanted to play again. He surprised me by refraining from asking me whether I would obey the rules now. The reason, I decided afterward, was that he knew, and I knew, there was no need to make a big issue of it. He just put his arm around my shoulders, gave me a gentle little hug and a pat on the back, and sent me into a game. That's all there was to it.

In spite of how simply it ended, that experience in its entirety represents the deepest and most profound experience anyone can ever have. For the first time in my life, I grasped what it meant to be loved. Though none of the other players ever gave any indication of a willingness to approve my behavior, all of them at various times indicated that they still loved me. In effect, they were telling me, "There are no conditions, no demands you have to meet, no expectations you have to meet in order for us to love you. But there are conditions, demands, and expectations you're going to have to come to terms with if you want us to include you in our games."

I got the message, and I knew I was absolutely free to accept or reject it. The consequences of each option were also clear—the joy of being included in the fun, or the misery of being excluded from the fun. I'd had to make up my mind whether or not to claim their love, and for three miserable weeks I had hatefully disdained their offer. I'd also had to make up my mind whether or not to accept the conditions for living together on a basketball court, and for three miserable weeks I had hatefully rejected that demand. As my misery increased during those weeks, it became clearer also that I could end it any time I chose to. And when I finally chose to claim their love and accept the conditions for living together, I was completely surprised by their openness and trust—no warnings, no lectures, and no probationary period—just an "understanding" that we all accepted.

At that time I grasped also what it meant to be forgiven. Forgiveness is such an important transaction among people like us who are always involved in wrongdoing. It is inevitable that finite people will do wrong, and it's important to admit to whatever specific wrongs we may commit, with the intent to correct our errant behavior as best we can. Forgiveness, then, is simply the willingness on the part of the wronged one to accept as sincere any wrongdoer's admission of error and intention to correct it. Obviously, what is involved here is more than a mere exchange of empty words. Rather, forgiving is a transaction that takes place at the deepest level of commitment and trust. For me that day on the basketball court, it was simply a deep, mutual understanding that was never put into words at all. And I was never more jubilant, and never more free.

While I have been emphasizing the need to limit the exercise of freedom in order to meet the conditions for living together harmoniously, I have also been suggesting indirectly that to love other people is to affirm their freedom to learn for themselves—through experiencing satisfying or painful consequences— how best to use their freedom. Only in this way do persons sharpen their own sensitivities, develop their capacities, and learn to stand on their own two feet.

A very simple, homey illustration will make this clear. Parents and other leaders must determine the readiness of other people to undertake given tasks, and to avoid calamity, they must then turn over that task to the one they've adjudged ready to handle it. The temptation we face is to avoid all risk of calamity, but in doing so we rob other people of the opportunity to learn and grow.

Now, another illustration. Douglas Steere writes that one Sunday afternoon, he and his wife were out for a walk in the little city of Deventer in Holland. When they drew near a large church, they saw that it had a long flight of stone steps—perhaps thirty or thirty-five of them—stretching from the street up to the entryway. A child about two years old had climbed those steps while his parents remained in the street below. Having reached the top, the child shouted with glee, but then he began calling for his father to come up and get him. The father refused, beckoning for the child to come down by himself. The child screamed, stamped his feet, and went into a rage, trying to coerce his father to come and get him. But the father continued to refuse.

Finally, the child cautiously put one foot down on the step below him and then slid his little bottom down onto it. Then, carefully, he put his foot down onto the step down and slid his bottom down onto it, and then the next and the next—one by one, slowly, painfully, descending those steps on his own. The parents waited expectantly, offering encouragement, anxiously sweating it out with the child until at last he had safely reached the sidewalk. Then the child was as delighted with himself as he had been on reaching the top, and, shouting with glee, ran at top speed into their arms. They hugged him warmly and, each taking a hand, went off together, a happy threesome.

The point is that love unfailingly affirms the free person each of us is, granting opportunity to develop whatever capacities each may have, willing to let each one fail if necessary in order to grow up. In love, one suffers *with* another through the learning process, offering appropriate encouragement but refusing to pamper.

In this connection, remember the father of the biblical prodigal son. I'm assuming here that the father had fulfilled his responsibility by discussing with his younger boy the possible consequences of "riotous living." But having done that, it would not have helped that boy simply to have gone and rescued him from the agony of his struggle with the pigs. He had to learn for himself those things he could not, or would not, learn without personal struggle. When he returned home, he discovered what it meant to be loved. He found that his father, without condoning his waywardness, was nevertheless happy to see him.

To love is to perceive the free being as precious, no matter how he or she exercises that freedom. Love is unconditional. It makes no demands and has no expectations that one must meet as a condition for being loved. That's a tough assignment, both in loving others and in loving oneself. But love is the strait gate and the narrow way that allows a person to learn for himself or herself what conditions are necessary for living in harmonious and satisfying relationships and in being content with oneself. And true love does not prevent anyone from experiencing the rewards or consequences of their choices.

CHAPTER TWENTY-TWO

Criticism

Summary: To love is to care so deeply about someone else that you risk sharing criticisms in order to improve the relationship, and to care so deeply for yourself that you accept criticism as an opportunity to improve.

Here's a recap of what we've learned so far.

I love you. "You" are priceless, no matter what kind of a body you have, no matter what kind of a mind you have, no matter what talents you have, no matter how you perform. You have no demands or expectations to meet as a condition for being loved. You are free—free to think your own thoughts, free to come to your own conclusions, and free to express yourself in any way you yourself may choose. Being free is precious, and to see you and affirm you as a free being is to love you.

But while there are no demands or expectations you have to meet as a condition for being loved, there are demands and expectations you must meet in order to live a peaceful, happy life. Through the consequences you experience as you use your freedom, you discover what those conditions are. The same is true for all of us.

Evaluation and criticism

Every expression of our freedom is being critically evaluated at every moment by the God of the universe, and it is reported to us in the experience of joy or pain, harmony or discord. I choose to call such critical evaluating and reporting *criticism*. In my way of thinking, it has a very positive value because it is the means God uses to help each of us to realize our full potential as individuals and to learn to relate to each other as members of a creative community. Any criticism God makes of our use of freedom is an expression of His love.

And criticism understood in this way is an expression of our love for each other. Because human brains, brawn, and talents are all finite, everything we do is imperfect. No matter who does what, there is always room for improvement. To offer specific suggestions for improving in this way or that is to criticize. As such, criticism is a very important aspect of learning—and especially so in the matter of learning how to live with each other in the nitty-gritty of everyday affairs, so that all derive maximum satisfaction from their interpersonal experience.

Caring

A common fallacy is to suppose that anyone who disagrees with our ideas or who disapproves of our actions doesn't love us. In reality, however, quite the opposite may be the case. Such confrontations may provide the only opportunity we have to evaluate our thoughts, attitudes, and behavior and to improve our lifestyle. The point is that criticism is one of the most important expressions of a loving attitude.

Consider Jesus' open honesty in speaking with the rich young ruler. When one is standing face-to-face with a man of great influence and power, there is always the temptation to hedge a bit in expressing one's honest feeling and opinions—if not to win his favor, at least to avoid his disfavor. But this man was obviously both vain and selfish. Should Jesus have ignored this fact in answering his question, "What do I need to do to experience this abundant life you're talking about?" Tact and diplomacy might have dictated that, and my guess is that Jesus' disciples would have favored such an approach. Think of all the prestige and prosperity this rich ruler could have added to their weak and struggling missionary cause!

Yet to ignore his vanity and selfishness in answering his question would have required Jesus not only to violate His own personal integrity but also to render a disservice to that young man. Only when others are honest enough with us to share openly and frankly their observations and opinions do we have an opportunity to evaluate our own stance and to make those adjustments that seem appropriate. I think it is significant that Jesus' reply, as recorded in the Gospel of Mark, is immediately preceded by the statement, "And Jesus, looking on him, loved him," as if to indicate that Jesus' words, "You'll have to become a lot more sensitive to the needs of people around you and put your mind and your money to work at the task of helping them," were an expression of love intended to meet that young man's deepest spiritual needs—a challenge to him to grow up to the level of spiritual maturity of which he was capable.

But notice that the challenge involved no pressure. It stood as a confronting choice, and at least as Jesus saw it, with abundant life hanging in the balance. Jesus affirmed him as a priceless person by sharing honestly what he thought and by recognizing that what the young ruler did with those comments was strictly up to him. However, there is the clear inference that that young man would have to assume personal responsibility for the consequences of whatever choice he made. There are demands and expectations that one has to meet as a condition for abundant living. There were demands and expectations at the time Jesus reportedly said to the scribes and Pharisees, "Don't you see how hypocritical it is to rob the poor in the temple and callously foreclose the mortgages on helpless widow's houses, and then turn right around and pretend to be righteous by paying tithes on all you make? In such behavior you actually ignore the weightier matters of the law—such as justice, mercy, and integrity—which are the only real measures of righteousness."

This young, upstart, itinerant preacher was speaking in this fashion to the "pillars of the church"—his elders and respected citizens of the community, men who were deeply religious and ardently devoted to the church. But such criticism is absolutely necessary if everyone is to find some satisfaction in the experience of living together. The leaders of the community must call for changes when the behavior of some members is causing pain. However, just as important, people ought to express appreciation when people's attitudes and actions contribute to the joy of living together. What is crucial in both cases is the spirit in which it is done.

The scribes and Pharisees need not have reacted in arrogance or hate because of Jesus' criticism of them. He wept for those men and expressed His disappointment at their rejection of His ministry: "If only I could help you to understand the truth upon which our well-being and peace depends," He lamented, "but you won't listen to Me." Such concern is a characteristic expression of love.

Attitude of love

Without such concern (sometimes even with it, but certainly without it), any critical evaluation suggesting another's need to change is inevitably perceived as moralistic rejection—because it *is* moralistic rejection. Without such deep caring for another's well-being and the well-being of the community, we have no right to voice our criticism. We must *first* restore the attitude of love in our own minds.

When we do care deeply, we must not keep still. He is no friend of mine—he doesn't love me—who knowingly allows me to continue to make the same mistakes and indulge in the same painful patterns without ever speaking to me about them. He does not love me—he fears me. She loves me who shares with me her impressions of how I cause pain and who supports my efforts to improve.

Concern courageous enough to confront is always one outcome of a loving attitude. Paul put it this way: "It is my hope that each of us within the community of the faithful may have such an experience of God's love as will enable all of us to reach maturity as measured by the full-statured development of the Christ."

There is no experience of God's love where there is no criticism. In fact, in the very same moment that I am perceived and affirmed as an immeasurably priceless person no matter what my behavior, I am simultaneously criticized by God through experiencing the consequences of my behavior. To be sensitive and responsive to both dimensions of this experience of God's love is my passport to growth.

What I am suggesting is that this is also the model for growth-producing experience in human relations, however imperfect our efforts may be. So I'd like to suggest three ways in which we might make our efforts to follow this model more effective.

How we can encourage growth

First, we can encourage growth by *becoming more precise in our expression of the meaning of love.* I can illustrate this from my own experience with my father.

I greatly admired my father, and as I was growing up, I know now I was really yearning for overt expressions of his love. But he didn't know what it meant to love, and neither did I. So we played the painful game of "salvation by works"—the game of seeking to win, earn, or buy approval for performance. I did everything I thought might earn some word of praise from him. But no matter what I said, he never gave me credit for being right, and no matter what I undertook, he always found some flaw to correct. He always had some suggestion as to how I could improve myself. Every evaluation had a "but" clause tacked on the end of it—tacked on "for my own good" as an expression of his duty to help me become the very best performer possible.

Such criticism, I now know, was not only quite appropriate but also extremely important. His duty was to help me grow up, and he did it well. What was lacking was the openly expressed assurance that I was appreciated as a precious person *regardless of flaws in my behavior.* All that ever got through to me was the cold certainty that no such warm assurance would ever be given until I became a perfect child. The rejection was subtle but real nevertheless, and for years and years after I left home, I was still striving to win or earn his love through my achievements in education and vocation. But the fact is that the most one can earn through such striving is approval for accomplishments—and that's not love.

What I was starved for were those experiences in our relationship that would have said to me, "Frank, you are precious to me just the way you are. You don't need to make any changes or any improvements for me to love you." I craved words like these openly expressed and overtly demonstrated. I'm sure I would have responded with something like, "Wow! That's exactly the way I see you: really precious to me despite all the obvious mistakes you make trying to be a good dad." That would have cleared the air. Then we could have gone to work helping each other to grow up by talking openly about our successes and our mistakes.

My point is that we tend either to be too unclear about what it really means to love or to be too stingy with our open and overt communication and demonstration of love. Thus, we have no solid ground to stand on as we evaluate our relationship with each other.

Second, we can do better at following the model of relating that God sets for us *by claiming the love actually offered to us.* So often, people whom other people are treating with love live as though that love were nonexistent. In the very presence of love, they perceive themselves to be unloved. In a variety of subtle ways they will dismiss the reality of being loved or rationalize it away. They always feel undeserving and unworthy of being loved, and at the same time they are always looking for reassurance that they are loved. However, all the reassurance in the world does them no good because they never claim the love that is offered. Obviously, in that state of mind they are so overly sensitive to criticism that they perceive the smallest suggestion to be rejection.

A young man who reacted like that felt depressed most of the time. One night, he was telling a group of friends how lonely he felt. He mentioned some lingering guilt over leaving the ministry, yet he could not tolerate the thought of going back just because he had been groomed for it from birth by his parents and the close-knit religious community in which he had grown up. He'd had an affair at one stage in his career, and he was certain that he wasn't the kind of husband or father he should be. Nor did he believe he was doing as well at work as he should have been. These and many other "failings" kept him depressed. Clearly, for him, love was something to be earned or deserved, and he wasn't good enough.

Despite all his imperfections, he seemed to be popular with his peers, his wife seemed devoted, and the members of the group warmly responded to him. That he *was loved* seemed obvious, yet he felt *un*loved—so lonely, so sensitive and defensive to the least criticism, so hurt that he kept trying to hide it all behind his whiskers and a wryly humorous front.

One night the group confronted him with his own unwillingness to accept the love offered him. When they did, he recognized and admitted that what they were saying was the case. He knew he was afraid to trust others to love him. The group challenged him to claim it right then and there in some symbolic act of his own choosing—from his wife, or his counselor, or from anyone or everyone in the group. We all waited in silence for him to act. As the minutes went by—close to twenty of them—the tension mounted. But when he finally claimed what had been there all along, he was born into a new era in his experience of life. Many changes followed, but what is pertinent here is that criticism that he previously had reacted to by falling into deep depression he now regarded as a challenge, an opportunity, a "happening" that triggered in him genuine possibilities for growth. He now knew that criticism of his behavior didn't necessarily mean rejection of his precious personhood. His being could be affirmed as precious at the same time that his performance was criticized as imperfect.

Third, do better at following the model of relating that God sets before us *by distinguishing the "self" that is immeasurably precious from those "expressions of the self" that have very temporary and limited value* because they are all imperfect in varying degrees. "I love you" means "I perceive *you* as precious." But the you that I see as precious is not to be identified with your performance. This is not to say that your performance is unimportant, but it is to say that you are precious no matter what kind of performance you put on.

I don't think it is possible to overemphasize the necessity for keeping these distinctions clearly in mind. Just see what happens when we don't: a preacher confuses the precious person he is with the lousy sermon he's just delivered, and since he has combined the two, when someone tells him the truth about his sermon, he feels worthless, rejected. Or a mother confuses the precious person she is with a poor meal she's just served, and since she has combined the two, when someone comments unfavorably on the meal, she feels put down, rejected. This kind of confusion could be illustrated ad infinitum—which points to the need to distinguish the priceless you from whatever equipment you have available (brains, brawn, talents) or any use you may make of it or any product that may result from your use of it.

The following thoughts, reviewed quietly, reflectively, in odd moments during each day, have proved helpful to many in making and maintaining this distinction.

> I am the Doer, but not the deed.
> I am the Thinker, but not the thought.
> I am the Speaker, but not the speech.
> I am the Correspondent, but not the letter.
> I am the Cook, but not the meal (and so forth).

True, I am responsible for both performance and product—no doubt about that—and I may need to make radical improvements in both. But I am precious even when my performance and products have questionable value. To keep that fact in perspective is to be open to criticism as an opportunity for growth.

To love and criticize at the same time and to *accept* love and criticism at the same time are very delicate and difficult functions that require genuine humility (in other words, a relaxed acceptance of one's own finiteness). But it is God's model for us, and it is the strait gate and narrow way that leads to our growth toward full maturity symbolized by the Christ.

CHAPTER TWENTY-THREE

Anger

Summary: Anger is a legitimate reaction to perceived hurt or rejection—the latter of which is a refusal by another to recognize and value us as intrinsically precious. Our anger, however, must be creatively controlled in order to preserve relationships and enhance personal and relational growth. Anger shows we have lost the attitude of love. We control our anger by restoring that attitude.

A brief review of what we've said so far. I love you. Love means to perceive a person to be precious just because and only because he or she is a human being. I love you means I perceive you to be precious. And obviously, if I perceive you to be precious, that perception is going to affect all my thinking about you and influence every conclusion I come to about you. Thus, it will determine the manner in which I relate to you.

The you that I'm seeing as precious is not your body. This is not to say that your body is not important, but it is to say that you are precious no matter what kind of body you may have. Your value is not determined by how closely your contours or facial features match our culture's idealized body image—nor by your sex or size or shape or age or color or state of health. None of these has anything to do with the fact—and it is a fact—that you are precious.

The you that I'm seeing as precious is not in your mind. This is not to say that your mind is not important, but it is to say that you are precious no matter what kind of mind you have. You are not the IQ that allows you to be mentally alert or limits you to slow dullness, and you are not a great reasoning ability or lack of it. These have nothing to do with the fact—and it is a fact—that you are precious.

Furthermore, it is not any particular skills, talents, or abilities that you have that make you precious. This is not to say that your special endowments are not important, but it is to say that you are precious no matter what potentials you may have. One talent or five or ten, it makes no difference because these have nothing to do with the fact—and it is a fact—that you are precious.

Actually, it is absolutely necessary that I go even a step further to say that the you I'm seeing as precious is not your performance. I have to admit, and it is something that is particularly emphasized in our achievement-oriented culture, that performance is important. But because its importance is so overemphasized, I must say with equal emphasis that you are precious no matter what kind of performance you put on. Not A's in school, not righteous behavior, not athletic prowess, not success or fame or fortune—none of these has anything to do with the fact—and it is a fact—that you are precious.

You are precious simply because you are. You were born that way. *To see that and to grasp the reality of it is to love.*

Harmonious relations and self-esteem seem possible only when that attitude is maintained. This universal law has been stated in many ways. The Jews, for example, articulated it as a simple and direct command of God: "You shall love your neighbor as yourself." The phrase *as yourself* correctly implies that love of self is a natural instinct. Every person senses that and acts to preserve it against any threat. More specifically, each of us is automatically defensive in the face of perceived rejection. To be ignored as though I do not exist, or to be treated as though I were worthless, is repulsive. Instinctively, spontaneously, I act to affirm the priceless nature of my own being by becoming angry and lashing back or, feeling very hurt, by withdrawing within a protective shell to guard the treasured me that I know I am.

But my reaction to being ignored or rejected also has a second purpose: to demand by angry words or pouting that others recognize the preciousness of the self I am and respond accordingly. Such demands fail because in making them I reject and ignore the very persons I want to love me. Once horns are locked in that way, the only solution is for one or the other of us, or both of us, to adopt an attitude of love—to see and affirm the other to be as precious as we are no matter how the others behave.

I have never met a human being who did not have these instinctive reflexes. To love oneself is a built-in reflex. Each of us is created to act that way.

To see what I have in mind, go with me in imagination to Jericho in Jesus' time. (This illustration is based on Luke 19:1–10.) Zacchaeus, a hated tax collector, has just heard of Jesus' approach to the city. Zacchaeus is a very short man, and he may very well have grown up hating his size. Imagine his memories of other children teasing him when he was a child—of the others sneering at him and calling him "runt," "squirt," "half-pint," or other derogatory names. Picked on, sometimes beaten up by bullies, he would run away and hide in his room. He often missed the fun of playing with other boys his age—they didn't want to be bothered with a runt like him. They said he wasn't good enough. This hurt Zacchaeus so deeply that he ached inside. Even his parents didn't seem to understand him, since they pushed, shoved, and prodded him into situations in which he was belittled. As a result, he became bitter and resentful of everyone.

So when the Romans offered him the job of tax collector, he took it. With that job he could get even. He could charge his tormentors whatever taxes he wished, and the Roman legionnaires would back him up.

In this way, Zacchaeus became rich and powerful. But he was miserable. The Jews considered him a traitor because he cooperated with the pagan Romans. Almost no one would walk with him in the street. Almost no one would have dinner with him. He was a lonely outcast, and his life was empty.

This, together with the knowledge that a former tax collector of his acquaintance was now one of Jesus' closest friends, must have lent a kind of desperation to Zacchaeus's desire to see Jesus. But by the time he arrived at the place where Jesus was, the crowd around Jesus made that impossible. He was too little! Would he be left out again? Desperate, Zacchaeus ran ahead, and, ignoring what little pride his position in that city gave him, he scrambled up into the lower branches of a sycamore tree like a child. He wanted to see this person he had heard would be a friend to anyone.

It's not hard to imagine how Zacchaeus must have felt when Jesus saw him and said he wanted to go to his home. A wild, delirious joy made Zacchaeus's heart pound as he fairly tumbled down out of the tree, half laughing, half crying. As they walked along together . . . But through our imaginations, I'll have Zacchaeus himself tell you what happened. Let's picture him as having written a letter to a fellow tax collector in Magdala. In it, he says,

> As we walked along toward the house, the crowd suddenly turned hostile and began deriding Jesus. "Going there to eat?" asked one.
>
> I heard the answer: "Oh, yes, He knows how to choose His table—the glutton."

"And His wine," said another. "Drunkard!"

He heard it as well as I, and my heart almost stopped beating. I could hardly stand the thought that He might change His mind about staying with me. But He reassured me with a smile, and a thrill of joy ran all through me. Yet my ears were burning, and my thoughts were all mixed up, for is it nothing, Johanon, after so long a time to be treated as a *person*? I had never felt that anyone really cared about *me* until that moment.

Suddenly, my heart was so full I blurted out, "Listen, I'll give my fortune back to the poor, and to anyone I have cheated I'll repay four times as much."

Then my tongue failed me. But He said, "God has found a home in your heart today, Zacchaeus."

All I can say is that I will never be the same again—old as I am, I am new.

Peace be with you,

Zacchaeus

Anger

Anger is the word I use to refer to the emotional reaction of a person to perceived rejection. Irritation, bitterness, resentment, hate, rage—whether mild or of great intensity, all are synonymous with anger as I use it here. Anyone who feels left out or deliberately shut out of a desired relationship with others automatically reacts with anger. Anger carries one message, simple and graphic: "Pay attention to me! I am precious, but you're not recognizing that fact, and it hurts so deeply I demand that you change." That's a very legitimate desire, and anger is a very legitimate emotion.

I think it is important to recognize that the way anger is handled determines how one relates with others. We move along a continuum from those who tend to bottle it up to those who tend to spew it out, from very withdrawn and submissive persons to very aggressive, dominant, violent individuals. Somewhere between these two extremes are those mature persons who recognize anger as the positive, self-affirming emotion it is and use the energy of anger in creative ways. With the energy it provides they correct their own inappropriate behavior and constructively confront others with the need to correct their behavior. That is, they do what can be done to correct whatever is causing the anger.

Spewing out anger and seeking revenge only perpetuate rejection and leave the offended person miserably lonely, empty, and discouraged. This is typical, and those who assert that getting out anger is a therapeutic experience ignore all the contrary evidence. They're simply lucky if someone happens along who is mature enough not to react by using the eye-for-an-eye and tooth-for-a-tooth approach but instead affirms the preciousness of the person despite her or his atrocious behavior. Most people never do the latter.

Jesus had that kind of maturity. Zacchaeus didn't have to meet any standards or measure up to any expectations in order to be loved. He made no conditions whatsoever. Jesus simply perceived and affirmed him as precious. That was it! And Zacchaeus knew then what it was to be loved.

Love's method

If it is destructive to spew out anger and equally destructive to bottle it up, how then can one handle it creatively?

One can handle it creatively by *restoring one's own attitude of love* without waiting for one's adversary to change. Angry people have lost the perspective of love. They are conditioning their love on other people's changing of their behavior. Angry people refuse to change their own hostile attitude until other people measure up to their expectations.

But we don't have to continue that pattern. We are not helpless victims of feelings of anger. We can change our feelings by changing our perception of the situation—in this instance, the precious nature of another person, no matter what their behavior may be. To do that is to restore the attitude of love. Appropriate feelings and behavioral changes will follow.

Every human being is responsible for maintaining or restoring that perspective. It would be easy to sympathize with angry people and censure those who have rejected and mistreated them, but let me emphasize that angry people can in no way escape their responsibility for their own attitude and behavior by blaming others. Remove the demands, and the feelings of pain and anger disappear. This first step in creative problem solving is absolutely indispensable.

At the risk of being repetitive but to eliminate possible confusion, it may be necessary here to point out that while no one can legitimately make demands of others as a condition for loving them, they may make *lots of legitimate demands on others as a condition for living and/or working with them.* It is essential that we grasp the fact that no conditions can be imposed on others as prerequisites for loving them! So I have no legitimate reason for staying hurt and angry. In fact, feelings of hurt and anger are the cue that I have lost the attitude of love. Feelings of hurt and anger confront me with my responsibility to restore the attitude of love immediately. When I am willing to eliminate all demands and expectations, feelings of hurt and anger will melt away. This opens the way for reasonable negotiations regarding any problem that arises in interpersonal living.

When we are angry, we are as responsible for adopting an attitude of love as are our detractors. Each of us is equally precious, and to see all those involved as such will affect all our thinking about them and influence for good every conclusion we come to concerning them. In the final analysis, it will determine the manner in which we relate to them. Who can say whether or not this will bring about a change in the attitude and behavior of our detractors? But we have no responsibility for that. Our responsibility is to maintain *our own* attitude of love and thus to keep the door open for discussion of those conditions necessary for living harmoniously with others.

In experimenting with this way of relating to his wife, a skeptical husband reported that he got up one morning before his wife and went into the bathroom to shave. After lathering up, he drew the razor down across his face—and felt as though he had pulled every whisker out by the roots. As usual, he exploded in anger, assuming that his wife had tampered with his razor—which actually was true; before she had gone to bed the previous night, she had used it to shave her legs.

The man recounted, "As I stormed out of the bathroom to wake up my wife and give her a tongue lashing, I remembered my commitment to experiment with trying to maintain an attitude of love. So I stopped in my tracks, still fuming, and thought about the demands I was making as a condition for my loving her. Realizing how precious she really was did something to me I wouldn't have believed possible. My anger seemed to just melt away. I knew that we still must discuss her use of my razor, but I wasn't angry at her anymore. I changed the blade and finished dressing, and when she got up, we came to a very reasonable understanding that I know from previous experience would not have been possible if I had blasted her awake with my anger."

APPENDIX

Life Sketch and Eulogy

Life Sketch

Shannon Marie Bigger was born in Burns, Oregon, on June 11, 1971. She was born into a family whose energies were focused on ministry and on people, and this focus shaped her life. Families involved in ministry tend to move a lot, and Shannon found her circle of experience widening rapidly. When she was nine years old, her family moved from Riverside, California, to College Place, Washington, where her father, Darold, became the senior pastor of the Walla Walla College Seventh-day Adventist Church. Shannon attended Rogers Elementary School and then Walla Walla Valley Academy, graduating from WWVA in 1990.

Shannon became active in ministry herself as she grew to adulthood. While a student at Walla Walla College, she served in the Campus Ministries program and volunteered for "Kids Connection," a monthly children's service at the college church. During the 1992–1993 school year, she spent a year as a Christian service volunteer on the island of Yap in the Federated States of Micronesia, where she taught first grade at the Yap Seventh-day Adventist school.

Her fellow parishioners at the Walla Walla College Church recognized her gift for ministry when they invited her to serve the congregation as an elder. A calling to ministry goes hand in hand with an interest in people, and Shannon was a "people person." In addition to her father's pastoral duties, Shannon's world included her mother, Barbara's, constant involvement with people as manager of the college store. Not surprisingly, Shannon chose to major in mass communications, which enabled her to reach out to many people in many ways, including ministry and service.

While a student at Walla Walla College, Shannon was an officer of the women's residence hall club, Aleph Gimel Ain, and she served as a resident assistant in the dormitory. She gained professional experience during those years by working as an announcer for KGTS-FM and Blue Mountain Television. She topped off her studies with a senior project at Walla Walla Valley Academy's Development office, where she started its first alumni newsletter.

After her college graduation in 1995, Shannon saw her circle of experience widening again—she moved to Takoma Park, Maryland, to serve as a development intern. Two weeks from when she was murdered, she was scheduled to return to the Northwest as the development director for Gem State Academy in Caldwell, Idaho. She died in Takoma Park on June 16, [1996].

In addition to her parents, Darold and Barbara, Shannon is survived by her sister Hilary, a senior social work major at Walla Walla College; her grandparents Forrest and Garnet Bigger, and Franklin and Marie Messinger; her great-grandmother Francis McCoy; many aunts, uncles, and cousins; and her foster sister, Rosemary Laraad from Yap, who joined the family in 1994.

Karen Johnson, Walla Walla College's vice president for development, read this sketch during the funeral. She had written it with the aid of Terri Aamodt.

Eulogy

Perhaps she [Shannon] first caught our attention when she was cast in the play *Inherit the Wind* as a schoolgirl, just some years ago. We doubt she saw herself as a burgeoning childhood actress in some way becoming famous, but it was a clue. She was a young lady of no ordinary craft, we discovered, already interested in language and in expressing herself and connecting with the souls of people. We weren't the first to see that.

"Here was a young girl," said one elementary teacher from Rogers School, "who delighted in the world of ideas, who was energized in the presence of others, who was serious about making something significant of her life."

"Even in those days she was clear on one issue," said the same teacher. "God would be central in her life." She willingly sought the counsel of God and others on the important matters of her life and chose to live by the highest principles—a lifestyle she saw modeled by her parents. Doesn't that fit your picture of Shannon?

"From an early age," said another elementary teacher, "she set about to do good. Kind, gentle, thoughtful, sensitive, perceptive—a sweet child," she concluded, "—an early believer."

During those elementary years, Shannon, Becky Duncan, Darlene Hintz, Tonya Jenks, and Wendy Johnson were a unit of their church early teen group that they called "The Pink Panthers." The girls had a great time together with their counselors, and when they moved on to high school, they decided that Shannon should keep their unit's scrapbook and "Ozzy," the stuffed pink panther mascot. They knew Shannon would cherish the memories of the activities they had shared together. So many of those traits proved to be right at the core of Shannon's character as she moved into high school and on.

"A caring person," said one academy staff member, "always upbeat."

"In fact," said the same person, "we happened to buy identical jackets while Shannon was at Walla Walla Valley Academy, and we'd wear them to basketball games by coincidence, and then we'd tell each other 'What good taste you have!' " Doesn't that fit your picture of Shannon?

I think we were waiting for Shannon when she enrolled in college in 1990. But she disarmed us, as evidenced by the reflections of so many of her peers. A student colleague, for example, who, like Shannon, did a year of student mission service, said: "The year I spent was full of so many tough times that I came back without a positive attitude at all. Soon after returning, I was sitting with Shannon, and she began asking me about my experience. While I recounted what had happened, she amazed me by systematically pointing out positive things that I had not seen before. That's how I remember Shannon. I never heard a negative word, tone, connotation, or inflection from her." Doesn't that fit your picture of Shannon?

"While on Yap," said another student colleague and volunteer, "I saw the impact she'd had there. Her students remembered her and were ecstatic when they learned that I was one of 'Ms. Bigger's' friends."

Back home, when one student began moving into the dorm one fall, Shannon gave her an assist in unloading the U-Haul trailer. When she did, she noticed a wall of shoes—"tens of pairs of them," admitted the new student. In the years that followed, the two—and others of them—came to spend thousands of happy hours together working at AGA and talking after Shannon did her night's check as the R.A., but they never forgot the U-Haul trailer and seventy boxes of shoes.

Recounted another, "Although she was a busy person with many friends and responsibilities, she never seemed too busy to listen. She loved to laugh, have fun, and," she added, "avoid homework."

"Shannon was the only person," mused yet another good friend, "who knew more about Mickey Mouse than I did."

One of the dorm deans, in fact, said quite candidly, "Shannon was a friend to me." Mature beyond her years, she was adventuresome; liked to try new things. She took a personal interest in each resident in her hall. In fact, on Shannon's last night as a resident R.A., she filed this report on the standard form and its questions: Cleanliness of the area? "Fine," reported Shannon, "—it's next to godliness." Evening contacts? Replied Shannon, "Actually, I wear them only from six to twelve A.M." Doesn't that fit your picture of Shannon?

Finally, some high praise from instructors in her major field. "The words that best describe Shannon," said one, "are *intelligent, reliable, dependable, caring, a sense of humor, one who laughed a lot, a good listener.* In class, where she sat right up front, she was a good student; she came prepared to discuss ideas, Christian beliefs, and how she saw herself and her writing talents fitting into the big picture of life."

Said a second, "Shannon had a strong feeling about what was right and wrong, and why. I can hear her say, 'But that's not fair!' She was very concerned," he concluded, "about fairness and justness."

"In her senior-level courses," observed a third, "she asked the questions teachers wished every student would ask. She was able to reason from cause to effect and then contribute significantly to thought discussions. Her research interests in fact and in writing put her on a par," said this instructor, "with graduate students. She made teaching a rewarding experience for us. With some students you could tell the day of the week, the amount of sleep and the level of stress, but not with Shannon. She looked as alert and well-dressed on the last class day as she did on the first—although in all candor, we do remember when she vented her inner self, and she did so on various occasions wherever two or three were gathered."

Said one more, "Occasionally, she'd pop into my office and ask how my day was. She would always brighten my day."

So *Inherit the Wind* may have been kind of a starting point for Shannon and some of us; it is though, not the ending point. We have every confidence that she will inherit the earth. Isn't that your picture of Shannon?

The eulogy was written and read by Loren Dickinson, who was a professor in the communication department and had been one of Shannon's instructors.

Forgive Now
Workshop

Darold Bigger and Barbara Hernandez have designed a workshop that explores the effects that forgiveness has on us physically, mentally, relationally, and spiritually. The *Forgive Now Workshop* shows how we can let go of even the most grievous offenses and experience peace and hope.

And if you can't bring Dr. Bigger and Dr. Hernandez to your hometown? What then?

How about doing the workshop yourself? Here's how you can.

The good doctors have recorded (live!) the eight presentations they make for the workshop. And they've written a coordinator's guide that, in addition to providing discussion questions and various other exercises, also offers suggestions on the mechanics of conducting the workshop.

There are handouts for the participants—worksheets for the discussion questions and the exercises and more. You can download them at no charge from the AdventistBookCenter. com Web site.

The four DVD set that contains the eight lectures plus the coordinator's guide cost $29.99. Order the set from your local Adventist Book Center, or call toll-free 1-800-765-6955, or go to AdventistBookCenter.com on the Internet.

P.S. While the *Forgive Now Workshop* was designed for groups, people can benefit by going through it individually too.